How to Turn Your Poker Playing Into a Business

Knowing What to Deduct to Improve Your Odds with the IRS

By

Ann-Margaret Johnston, CPA

Abacus Enterprises, LLC

www.pokerdeductions.com

How to Turn Your Poker Playing into a Business

Copyright © 2005, Ann-Margaret Johnston

Abacus Enterprises, LLC

Design work by Susan Daniel Creatives, Inc.

Photography by Mike Powell

Printing by Matthews Printing Company

ISBN # 0-9774862-0-6

TABLE OF CONTENTS

DEDICATION

To my wonderful husband, David, who has supported my ideas and has always encouraged my drive for success. I am so thankful for the day I met you. I am also thankful that you will never know how much money I have lost playing poker!

ACKNOWLEDGEMENT

This book would not be possible without the encouragement from my family, friends and clients. I first want to thank Ben for his advice over the years and letting me bother him with countless accounting questions as my business grew. Thanks also goes to Steph for loving my book idea and believing in me – a true friend for life, my staff who has helped to type, proofread and encourage me, to Kelly who had to pick up the "slack" at the office, to Hot Rod for the chips and the chair and to my Rotary club for letting me brag-a-buck more than most. Also, to my parents for the "accident" that occurred in 1967 when the plan was retiring and not parenting.

Finally, I want to thank all of the poker players over the years that took my money so that I would quickly realize that I better stick to accounting for a living!

DISCLAIMER

Reasonable care has been taken in preparing this book. Readers are cautioned that this book is sold with the understanding that the author is not engaged in rendering legal, accounting or other professional services within this text.

This book is for informational purposes only and to be used as a guide based on your personal tax situation. The author does not suggest or imply that readers avoid paying taxes that are legally owed to the government. The author has no liability or responsibility to anyone that directly or indirectly uses information in this book. In addition, this book is based on the information available at the time of publication. Some information may change after publication and author disclaims any responsibility for those changes. The information contained herein only relates to Federal tax law. The laws on tax preparation for your State may vary.

Readers with specific tax problems, questions, or issues are urged to seek the professional advice of a tax accountant, tax preparer or an attorney.

INTRODUCTION

Due to the recent popularity of poker that is sweeping the nation, I decided to write a book to assist those that want to take a leap of faith and become a professional poker player as well as to help those who are "casual" players know what to do with their winnings. I also wanted to help people understand the tax difference in being a professional player and gambling as a hobby.

I realize that tax information is difficult to understand. Very few people are able to explain it so that the average person can grasp its meaning. I have tried to bring the information "down to earth" and take the confusing terminology out and show the basic rules. My goal is to have the information available that would normally be difficult for people to find on their own. As we all know, tax information is rarely "cut and dry". Just when you think you know the answer, the rules change. Ask any accountant a difficult question and the most common answer is "it depends". With that as the answer, the questions are rarely answered with any certainty. When talking to accountants, you tend to be even more confused after your conversation than you were before you started! I want to try to change that.

Although the information contained herein applies to all forms of gambling/gaming, I am focusing specifically on poker – from brick and mortar casinos to internet to home games. As the craze increases due to the television response, and more unknown players become World Champions, people wonder if they can turn their skills into a lucrative living or should they be happy playing as a hobby.

I really wanted to give people the information they need to help them with their tax questions. The biggest question that I hear is what deductions can you take and how do you report all of this to the IRS. It's confusing but can truly be broken down to where it doesn't feel like a foreign language. I feel that I have always had the ability to simplify tax information to my clients throughout the years and add a personality to it. My hope is that you will be armed with the information that can help you to tackle this difficult subject.

I've been playing poker for about 7 years and fell in love with the game from the start. I realized that even though I had a love of the game and the passion to play, I'd never have the time, patience or ability to be a pro. I decided by writing this book, I can continue my two passions – Poker and Accounting.

A CHIP AND A CHAIR

♠ ♥ ♣ ♦

"Well, I know what I want to do the rest of my life," I said to my husband with a grin. "And what would that be?" he replied.

I laid $2,000 dollars on the bed of our Vegas hotel room. I had started with $100.

"Whoa, what happened to you?" he asked.

"I turned $100 into $2,000 in 8 hours – this game sure beats doing tax returns! The way I figure it, if I could make $1,500 a day, 5 days a week for 50 weeks that is $375,000 a year. And, I can have fun at the same time!"

"Beginners luck," he said. "Let's see how much you have 4 days from now when we are ready to head home."

Four days later and a $500 withdrawal from the ATM, I decided I better keep my day job.

So, you think you can take your poker skills, quit your job, and become a professional poker player? Ten years ago people would think you are crazy, roll their eyes and wish you a lot of luck. Well, today it's not such a crazy idea. With the increased popularity of poker, no matter where you live, you can find a poker game – be it in a restaurant or on your computer.

Poker is exploding and with it comes a lot of questions on how to proceed financially. Players are becoming so serious about playing that they are now hiring agents and managers. With the ever-growing prize pools, people are getting the opportunity to change their lives by playing poker.

The dream of being a professional athlete is seldom a reality. It takes the right physical characteristics to be a Michael Jordan or a Mohammad Ali. Luck and cash don't really make you a star Quarterback. But, do you want to be a professional poker player and make millions? It is not impossible. With patience, skill and a little luck, you can make a living from this phenomenon.

Most people are introduced to the game from television. They also are practicing this new skill on the internet, where you can play 10 hours a day and make thousands of dollars from wherever you may live. It is truly unbelievable what is happening and the tremendous amount of money that you can make without leaving the comfort of your home. Talk about a home-based business! Before you know it, stay at home moms could make more than their 9-5 husbands!

Playing at a brick and mortar casino is now easier than ever. It used to be that you had to go to Las Vegas and Atlantic City to play poker. Now, casinos are sprouting up everywhere. If there isn't a casino in your State, it is sure to be up for discussion by legislators in the near future. In addition, tournaments are everywhere. Bars and restaurants in States that do not allow gambling are able to skirt around the rules.

The prize pools for tournaments are astounding everyone. No-name players are becoming famous overnight. Just turn on the television and there is a tournament where someone else has suddenly become a millionaire. And lately the average player is foregoing the large buy-ins by "winning" seats for as little as $30 on the internet. There is certainly room at the top in the poker world and the number of entries in tournaments is increasing exponentially.

So what does this mean to you? It means that if you are earning and/or losing money from poker, the IRS may very well come into play. The question is what to do, and how and what to report to the government.

Knowing when you can call your poker playing a business is the key to both tax savings and tax compliance. Many of us love to play for fun but when you start to consistently win – and especially when you win big – you need to know how this will affect your tax situation. Even when you are a casual player and don't want to be a business, there are things you need to know about how this impacts your tax return. Just because your losses more than offset your wins, it does not mean that you do not have a potential tax reporting obligation.

The first important determination is whether you are playing poker as a hobby or a business. Once that is established, then the path you take will be clearer on how to proceed with your tax situation. The rules are the same and yet they are different. Read on to learn more.

DOING IT FOR LOVE OR MONEY?
(ARE YOU A HOBBY OR A BUSINESS?)

♠ ♥ ♣ ♦

I decided to move down to the $5/$10 table since my run on cards went cold. I sat down next to a guy that was just starting to reach in his pocket for more cash. Good, I thought, maybe he is on tilt and I can pick up some extra money.

He wore a hat with a matching t-shirt of a popular internet poker site. He even had a matching jacket. To his detriment, he had "rookie" written all over him. I could swear that he had pimples on his face!

When he was first to act after the flop and declared "raise" several of us shot glances at each other. After a few more hands, he started to show off to me about how the guy in the #2 position didn't know what he was doing.

He started to strike up a conversation with me. "So, what do you do for a living?" he asked. "I have a CPA firm," I replied. "What about you?"

"As soon as I get enough of a bank roll, I plan to turn pro," he announced. "Wow," I said, acting as if that was impressive.

"So," he said, "I am ahead of the game because I have started to treat my poker as a business now before I turn pro. I am really planning to write off every move I make."

"Sorry, I don't think you can do that," I replied. I then gave him some advice on the difference between a hobby and a business. He turned a little pale. I wasn't sure if it was what I said or the boat that beat his flush.

We all want to make a living doing what we enjoy. So many times we choose a job that is geared more toward income potential rather than what we love to do. We also are influenced by our family and peers as to what is considered a "respectable" job. We tend to do our jobs to earn a living and then take up a hobby in order to have fun.

The majority of people have a job and a separate hobby because they feel that you can't have fun and make money at the same time. We all know the person that has tried to turn their hobby into a business and have failed miserably. Just because you love animals doesn't mean you can make a lucrative living running a pet store. Luckily, the "new" world of poker can allow you to either play as a hobby or turn it into a business. Either way, you usually have a lot of fun with it.

So, what is the difference? A hobby is an activity for which you do not expect to make a profit. If you are thinking of starting a business but it does not provide you with the ability to earn a living, or to make a profit, it very well may be a hobby.

It is important to first distinguish as to what your intentions are with your poker playing. Ask yourself these questions:

- How often do you play?

- Do you depend on these winnings to pay bills?

- Do you have another job and if so, how many hours per week do you work?

- How much time do your dedicate to playing poker?

The answers to these questions are important. A hobby is something you usually do in your spare time and is not relied upon to pay the bills. It is normally for fun or entertainment in addition to your other main income source. Profit is not typically the main goal when you have a hobby.

It is important to know the difference between something that is a hobby and something that is for profit. Hobby expenses are deductible only to the extent of hobby income.

> **NOTE: Gambling expenses, if you are a hobby, are treated differently from any other hobby. Non-professional gamblers are not allowed to deduct expenses for transportation, meals, lodging, etc. You can only offset your income with the money you lose.**

The IRS has several "facts and circumstances" tests in making the distinction between a hobby and a business. Unfortunately no one factor necessarily helps to determine this.

The following are factors that should normally be taken into account:

- Whether you carry on the activity in a businesslike manner

- Whether the time and effort you put into the activity indicate you intend to make it profitable

- Whether you depend on income from the activity for your livelihood

- Whether your losses are due to circumstances beyond your control (or are normal in the start-up phase of your type of business)

- Whether you change your methods of operation in an attempt to improve profitability

- Whether you, or your advisors, have the knowledge needed to carry on the activity as a successful business

- Whether you were successful in making a profit in similar activities in the past

- Whether the activity makes a profit in some years, and how much profit it makes

- Elements of personal pleasure or recreation

The IRS guidelines on this topic are available in Section 1.183-2 (a) and (b) of the Federal tax regulations which is a great topic to read if you are an insomniac!

So, let's talk about those "facts and circumstances". In plain English, Sec 1.183-2(a) says that all of these facts and circumstances are taken into account on a case by case basis when the IRS tries to determine if you are a business. Although a reasonable expectation of profit is not required, the facts and circumstances must indicate that the taxpayer entered into the activity with the objective of making a profit. In determining whether an activity is engaged in for profit, greater weight is given to the facts rather than the taxpayer's mere intent. What does this mean? It means it is up to the IRS for the final determination if your return is examined and your intent is questioned.

The following briefly describes the "relevant factors" in the facts and circumstances list:

BUSINESSLIKE MANNER

What is a "businesslike" manner? This means that you need to conduct yourself like any other type of business. You need to maintain books and records as well as receipts. One recommendation is to have a business plan. Where this sounds complicated, it really isn't. Write it out by hand if you want, it does not have to be formal or fancy. It is really a good idea to have this if ever challenged by the IRS. This shows that you went into your business with a thought-process on how it is going to be profitable.

The following topics should be in a business plan:

- **The Company** – Background information on yourself and any investors, and how the company is structured.
- **Product/Service** – Describe what you do, potential profitability of what you do, and competitive advantages that you may have over others in this type of business.
- **Market Analysis** – Summary of the industry, the amount of earning potential, areas to generate profit and any advertising markets. Also include any potential pitfalls that may occur.
- **Finance** – The money that you have to start with and any cash needs that may arise. Also include profit forecasts as well as anticipated expenses. It is best to forecast out revenue and expenses for the period of one year.

- **Future Endeavors** – Describe if you have areas that you may want to go into or any projects that may be in a possibility the future. List profit centers that you could possibly branch out into one day.
- **Team Players** – List everyone that is and could be involved in your business and the role that they may play in your success.

TIME AND EFFORT

The IRS looks to see if you devote most of your personal time and effort to the activity. Also, if you leave one occupation to devote most of your time and energy to the activity, it provides evidence that you are doing this for profit. The number of hours you spend and the result you achieve is a good indicator.

LIVELIHOOD

The fact that you depend on this activity to be successful is important. If you do not have income from other sources, it is also a good indicator that you are engaged in this for profit. Its fine to have other sources of income, however, substantial income from other sources could indicate that this is just for recreation and not for profit.

LOSSES BEYOND YOUR CONTROL

Incurring losses when you first start a business is understandable and does not necessarily mean that you are not engaged in it for a profit. However, if you have several years of losses without any profits, you are at risk. Each situation is different and if you have unforeseen circumstances, this is taken into account.

CHANGING YOUR METHODS TO IMPROVE PROFIT

If you continue to incur losses, you need to either find another business or have a plan on how to change your operations. Otherwise, you are at risk that you are not truly in business for profit.

KNOWLEDGE OF THE BUSINESS TO BE SUCCESSFUL

Preparing for the activity by studying the industry and consulting with experts in the field help to indicate there is a profit motive. Conversely, when someone does the preparation but does not carry on the activity properly, this may lack intent to derive profit.

SUCCESS IN THE PAST

Perhaps if you have engaged in similar activities in the past and have now changed things to where you have become profitable. Even though you may have some unprofitable years, this may indicate that it is presently engaged for profit.

PROFIT IN SOME YEARS

If you have losses but have a series of years where net income is realized, you have strong evidence that you are in the business for a profit. An activity is presumed to be for profit if it produced a profit in at least 3 of the last 5 tax years. If your business activity passes this profit test, the IRS will usually assume it is carried on for profit.

ELEMENTS OF PERSONAL PLEASURE

This is the scary part for gamblers. The IRS feels that the presence of personal motives in carrying on an activity may indicate that it is not engaged in for profit. On the other hand, the fact that the taxpayer gets pleasure out of the activity is not sufficient to cause the activity to be considered a hobby.

Confused? It's really just a function of holding yourself out there as a true trade or business. It doesn't mean you can't have fun at the same time. It does mean, however, that it needs to be treated seriously. Just be careful to read the facts and circumstances. The IRS does not have a firm set of rules so, as I said previously, it is a case by case basis. Just have your bases covered!

Remember that gambling is in a field that tends to be more scrutinized than other professions. The IRS actually holds professional gamblers to a very high standard. The history of gambling has not been favorable in the eyes of the IRS. There has always been a moral opposition and the Courts have been known to put gambling winnings with thievery. The IRS looks at professional gambling with more skepticism so it is important to be very cautious in your determination of a business or a hobby.

So, let's examine other criteria for a business. To pursue poker as a business, you need to dedicate it as a full-time job. You need to derive the majority of your income from your winnings. Having another job, in my opinion, is not a good idea. Again, the rules are not set in stone but how you conduct yourself could cause the IRS to determine that you are a hobby. This could be a major problem as the reporting requirements and the tax treatment differ tremendously.

There was a well known court case that addressed several issues, mainly the issue of whether gambling can be considered a trade or business. The case was Commissioner v. Groetzinger, 480 U.S. which says:

For gambling to reach the level of a trade or business activity, it must be "pursued full time, in good faith, and with regularity, to the production of income for a livelihood, and is not a mere hobby."

There have been more and more court cases involving gamblers in the past several years since the Groetzinger case that have accepted gambling as a trade or business. Because of these cases, gambling as a business is more acceptable than in the past.

I'M IN IT FOR LOVE, NOW WHAT?

♠ ♥ ♣ ♦

It is January and my husband has a business meeting in Wisconsin. I have never been there so I decided to go along. Unfortunately, I am not ready for temperatures of negative 18 degrees Fahrenheit.

We checked in at the Bed and Breakfast and immediately go to a display showing "things to do" in the area. I begin to pray for a nearby casino and I am in luck.

It is a short 45 minute drive in the country and then I arrive on an Indian Reservation. I was so excited to see the large sign that I didn't realize I was doing 50mph in a 25 mile "Indian Reservation zone". I quickly learned the Federal laws but luckily used my Southern charm to get a warning. I was hoping that was not an indication of my luck for the rest of the day.

The poker room was small and the only game is $2/$4 limit. I sat down to play and noticed that almost everyone is a local. Most people playing were American Indians except for me and one other older gentleman.

Steven is on my right and everyone is congratulating him on his $5,000 tournament win last week.

The conversation turns to a joke about claiming income. He says "Well, they gave me one of those W2G Forms so I will just tell the IRS that I had the same amount for my losses."

"Do you play for a living?" I ask. "Nope," he replied, "just something I enjoy doing on the weekends. I love to play and I especially like winning tournaments. If they had not given me that stupid form, I wouldn't have to deal with the tax mess." "Don't let the IRS hear you say that!" I said.

Many gamblers, be it casual or not, do not report their winnings and losses if the net is a loss. Many more only report the amount from a Form W2G and offset the exact amount on their Schedule A if they are a hobby. That is fine if that is a true representation, but you better make sure you can back up those losses. (See Chapter 8) Unfortunately, if you can not itemize on your return, you might lose those losses as a deduction.

Here is why it is important – the case of Judge Scholl. Yes, that's right, the IRS was auditing an Arizona Superior Court Judge. The Judge lost and he appealed and here is what happened.

Judge Scholl was a gambler who reported gambling winnings and losses. He reported the exact same amount for his winnings and his losses on his 1987 tax return. On his 1988, 1990 and 1993 returns, he did not reflect any gambling wins or losses and his 1991, 1992 and 1994 returns reflected only small amounts that happened to be the exact amount that was reported to him on a Form W2G.

Scholl testified that he thought he could "net out" his gambling wins & losses and if losses exceeded wins, nothing needed to be reported on the return. The end result is that the jury found that he willfully failed to report both gambling income and gambling losses. The Court of Appeals upheld the conviction. (US vs. Scholl, No. 97-10143, 97-10248)

The problem is that many gamblers think that because you have enough losses to offset winnings, there is no reason to report either to the IRS. **YOU CANNOT NET THESE TOGETHER AND NOT REPORT THEM!**

Remember, it becomes a criminal offense to sign a tax return that is incorrect and untrue. If the IRS can prove that you had intent to violate the law, this is considered fraud. Then life gets really ugly for you with the government. If they determine fraud, there is no statute of limitations. What this means is that the IRS can look back to the first day that you ever filed a tax return.

The average person will go to a casino, play, win some, (usually) lose more, and then go home. If you are not a professional gambler, the wins must be reported on the front page of your 1040, on the line that says "Other income. List type and amount." This is called hobby income, specifically from gambling, and yes, you are required to report it.

Hobby income is not subject to Self-employment tax. Self-employment tax is Social Security (6.2%) and Medicare (1.45%) and then you have to match it. Therefore, Self-employment tax is 15.3% of your net income. A person that has their own business has to pay this tax in addition to Federal income tax on their net income (and any state tax, if applicable). But, if you are a hobby, this is not the case.

Although income from a hobby is not subject to Self-employment tax, it is taxed for Federal income tax, depending on your tax bracket. That is the good news. The bad news (possibly) is that the losses that can offset hobby income cannot be netted on the front page of your 1040 on the line that says "Other income. List type and amount." The losses to offset that income can only be deducted on a Form called a Schedule A. This form is for itemized deductions.

Here is the bad part of all this. If you cannot itemize, you technically cannot offset those gambling winnings. It's unfair but it's the rule. If you have a substantial amount of losses, i.e. over about $5,000, then you may be able to itemize with just your gambling losses.

So you do not know if you can itemize or you have no clue what this means? Basically, the IRS lets you take a "standard deduction" on your return or you can itemize your deductions. The standard deduction amount depends on if you are single, married filing joint, married filling separate, head of household, or if you are a qualifying widow. The IRS lets you use the greater of the standard deduction or the itemized amount for the most tax benefit.

How do you know which amount could be higher? You will want to calculate the numbers and see. Most people that itemize have the following expenses:

- Large amounts of out of pocket medical expenses
- Pay property taxes on a home/land, etc.
- Have State tax withheld or paid in during the year
- Large purchases where sales tax was paid
- Have a mortgage and pay interest on that mortgage
- Have made both cash and non-cash contributions (clothing and other similar donations)
- Have a substantial amount of business expenses that have not been reimbursed
- Gambling losses

The above items are some of the frequently itemized deductions. There are more deductions that can add to the total. The best way to know is look at Schedule A and the instructions to better understand what could help you make this determination. They both can be found at the IRS website at www.irs.gov. My website at **www.pokerdeductions.com** has a link to this site.

Again, if you see that the standard deduction amount is higher after adding these items together, then it is in your best interest to use the standard deduction amount.

Unfortunately, you don't entirely reap the benefits of your gambling losses. And, to add insult to injury, if your income is really high, and you can itemize, the itemized deductions get limited! Feels like you literally can't "win," doesn't it?! The standard deduction numbers change each year. You can find these amounts on the IRS website.

Here is an example of a tax situation and how to prepare the return.

EXAMPLE 1 – TAX RETURN

Ben Smith is a single guy with no dependents that went to Vegas to play poker about 4 times last year. He has a regular job where he had the following reported on his Form W2:

Wages, tips and other compensation	$50,000
Social Security withheld	3,100
Medicare withheld	725
Federal withheld	10,000
State withheld	2,000

He was given a Form W2G for a tournament he won showing $10,000 but won a lot more money than what the Form showed. He kept up with his other winnings which were another $3,000. He also kept up with his losses which were about $2,500 at the tables. His trips to Vegas totaled $3,000 for hotel and airfare. He rents an apartment and had no charitable contributions, medical expenses or any other deductions that could be itemized. The standard deduction for this particular tax year is $5,000 and the amount per exemption is $3,200.

The following is the way he would prepare his tax return.

How To Turn Your Poker Playing Into A Business

Example 1:

Form **1040**	U.S. Individual Income Tax Return		(99)	IRS Use Only - Do not write or staple in this space.		OMB No. 1545-0074

For the year Jan. 1-Dec. 31, , or other tax year beginning , ending , 20

Label (See instructions on page 16.) — L A B E L

Use the IRS label. Otherwise, please print or type. — H E R E

Your first name and initial	Last name	Your social security number
BEN	SMITH	007 07 0007

If a joint return, spouse's first name and initial	Last name	Spouse's social security number

Home address (number and street). If you have a P.O. box, see page 16.	Apt. no.	▲ **Important!** ▲
99955 HEART CLUB DRIVE		You **must** enter your SSN(s) above.

City, town or post office, state, and ZIP code. If you have a foreign address, see page 16.
DIAMOND, GA 77733

Presidential Election Campaign (See page 16.) ▶ Note. Checking "Yes" will not change your tax or reduce your refund.
Do you, or your spouse if filing a joint return, want $3 to go to this fund? ▶ You: [ ] Yes [X] No   Spouse: [ ] Yes [ ] No

Filing Status
Check only one box.

1 [X] Single
2 [ ] Married filing jointly (even if only one had income)
3 [ ] Married filing separately. Enter spouse's SSN above and full name here. ▶
4 [ ] Head of household (with qualifying person). (See page 17.) If the qualifying person is a child but not your dependent, enter this child's name here. ▶
5 [ ] Qualifying widow(er) with dependent child (see page 17)

Exemptions

6a [X] Yourself. If someone can claim you as a dependent, **do not** check box 6a .... Boxes checked on 6a and 6b: **1**
b [ ] Spouse ....
c Dependents:
(1) First name Last name	(2) Dependent's social security number	(3) Dependent's relationship to you	(4) ✓ if qualifying child for child tax credit (see page 18)

No. of children on 6c who:
● lived with you
● did not live with you due to divorce or separation (see page 18)

Dependents on 6c not entered above

If more than four dependents, see page 18.

d Total number of exemptions claimed .... Add numbers on lines above ▶ **1**

Income

Attach Form(s) W-2 here. Also attach Forms W-2G and 1099-R if tax was withheld.

If you did not get a W-2, see page 19.

Enclose, but do not attach, any payment. Also, please use Form 1040-V.

			Amount
7	Wages, salaries, tips, etc. Attach Form(s) W-2	7	50,000.
8a	Taxable interest. Attach Schedule B if required	8a	
b	Tax-exempt interest. Do not include on line 8a	8b	
9a	Ordinary dividends. Attach Schedule B if required	9a	
b	Qualified dividends (see page 20)	9b	
10	Taxable refunds, credits, or offsets of state and local income taxes	10	
11	Alimony received	11	
12	Business income or (loss). Attach Schedule C or C-EZ	12	
13	Capital gain or (loss). Attach Schedule D if required. If not required, check here ▶ [ ]	13	
14	Other gains or (losses). Attach Form 4797	14	
15a	IRA distributions 15a	b Taxable amount (see page 22)	15b	
16a	Pensions and annuities 16a	b Taxable amount (see page 22)	16b	
17	Rental real estate, royalties, partnerships, S corporations, trusts, etc. Attach Schedule E	17	
18	Farm income or (loss). Attach Schedule F	18	
19	Unemployment compensation	19	
20a	Social security benefits 20a	b Taxable amount (see page 24)	20b	
21	Other income. List type and amount (see page 24) GAMBLING WINNINGS 13,000.	21	13,000.
22	Add the amounts in the far right column for lines 7 through 21. This is your **total income** ▶	22	63,000.

Adjusted Gross Income

23	Educator expenses (see page 26)	23	
24	Certain business expenses of reservists, performing artists, and fee-basis government officials. Attach Form 2106 or 2106-EZ	24	
25	IRA deduction (see page 26)	25	
26	Student loan interest deduction (see page 28)	26	
27	Tuition and fees deduction (see page 29)	27	
28	Health savings account deduction. Attach Form 8889	28	
29	Moving expenses. Attach Form 3903	29	
30	One-half of self-employment tax. Attach Schedule SE	30	
31	Self-employed health insurance deduction (see page 30)	31	
32	Self-employed SEP, SIMPLE, and qualified plans	32	
33	Penalty on early withdrawal of savings	33	
34a	Alimony paid b Recipient's SSN ▶	34a	
35	Add lines 23 through 34a	35	
36	Subtract line 35 from line 22. This is your **adjusted gross income** ▶	36	63,000.

410001 11-03-04

LHA For Disclosure, Privacy Act, and Paperwork Reduction Act Notice, see page 75.   Form **1040**

Example 1:

Form 1040	BEN SMITH		007-07-0007			Page 2

Tax and Credits

Standard Deduction for -
- People who checked any box on line 38a or 38b **or** who can be claimed as a dependent.
- All others:

Single or Married filing separately, $4,850

Married filing jointly or Qualifying widow(er), $9,700

Head of household, $7,150

Line	Description		Amount
37	Amount from line 36 (adjusted gross income)	37	63,000.
38a	Check { You were born before January 2, 1940, ☐ Blind. } **Total boxes** if: { Spouse was born before January 2, 1940, ☐ Blind. } **checked** ▶ 38a		
b	If your spouse itemizes on a separate return or you were a dual-status alien, see page 31 and check here ▶ 38b ☐		
39	**Itemized deductions** (from Schedule A) or your **standard deduction** (see left margin)	39	5,000.
40	Subtract line 39 from line 37	40	58,000.
41	If line 37 is $107,025 or less, multiply $3,100 by the total number of exemptions claimed on line 6d. If line 37 is over $107,025, see the worksheet on page 33	41	3,200.
42	**Taxable income.** Subtract line 41 from line 40. If line 41 is more than line 40, enter -0-	42	54,800.
43	**Tax.** Check if any tax is from: a ☐ Form(s) 8814 b ☐ Form 4972	43	10,444.
44	**Alternative minimum tax.** Attach Form 6251	44	
45	Add lines 43 and 44 ▶	45	10,444.
46	Foreign tax credit. Attach Form 1116 if required	46	
47	Credit for child and dependent care expenses. Attach Form 2441	47	
48	Credit for the elderly or the disabled. Attach Schedule R	48	
49	Education credits. Attach Form 8863	49	
50	Retirement savings contributions credit. Attach Form 8880	50	
51	Child tax credit (see page 37)	51	
52	Adoption credit. Attach Form 8839	52	
53	Credits from: a ☐ Form 8396 b ☐ Form 8859	53	
54	Other credits. Check applicable box(es): a ☐ Form 3800 b ☐ Form 8801 c ☐ Specify	54	
55	Add lines 46 through 54. These are your **total credits**	55	
56	Subtract line 55 from line 45. If line 55 is more than line 45, enter -0- ▶	56	10,444.

Other Taxes

57	Self-employment tax. Attach Schedule SE	57	
58	Social security and Medicare tax on tip income not reported to employer. Attach Form 4137	58	
59	Additional tax on IRAs, other qualified retirement plans, etc. Attach Form 5329 if required	59	
60	Advance earned income credit payments from Form(s) W-2	60	
61	Household employment taxes. Attach Schedule H	61	
62	Add lines 56 through 61. This is your **total tax** ▶	62	10,444.

Payments

If you have a qualifying child, attach Schedule EIC.

63	Federal income tax withheld from Forms W-2 and 1099	63	10,000.		
64	2004 estimated tax payments and amount applied from 2003 return	64			
65a	**Earned income credit (EIC)**	65a			
b	Nontaxable combat pay election ▶ 65b				
66	Excess social security and tier 1 RRTA tax withheld (see page 54)	66			
67	Additional child tax credit. Attach Form 8812	67			
68	Amount paid with request for extension to file (see page 54)	68			
69	Other payments from: a ☐ Form 2439 b ☐ Form 4136 c ☐ Form 8885	69			
70	Add lines 63, 64, 65a, and 66 through 69. These are your **total payments** ▶		70	10,000.

Refund

Direct deposit? See page 54 and fill in 72b, 72c, and 72d.

71	If line 70 is more than line 62, subtract line 62 from line 70. This is the amount you **overpaid**	71	
72a	Amount of line 71 you want **refunded to you** ▶	72a	
b	Routing number ▶ ▶ c Type: ☐ Checking ☐ Savings d Account number ▶		
73	Amount of line 71 you want **applied to your 2005 estimated tax** ▶	73	

Amount You Owe

74	**Amount you owe.** Subtract line 70 from line 62. For details on how to pay, see page 55 ▶	74	444.
75	Estimated tax penalty (see page 55)	75	

Third Party Designee Do you want to allow another person to discuss this return with the IRS (see page 56)? ☐ **Yes.** Complete the following. ☐ **No**
Designee's name ▶ Phone no. ▶ Personal identification number (PIN) ▶

Sign Here
Under penalties of perjury, I declare that I have examined this return and accompanying schedules and statements, and to the best of my knowledge and belief, they are true, correct, and complete. Declaration of preparer (other than taxpayer) is based on all information of which preparer has any knowledge.

Joint return? See page 17. Keep a copy for your records.

Your signature	Date	Your occupation	Daytime phone number
Spouse's signature. If a joint return, **both** must sign.	Date	Spouse's occupation	

Paid Preparer's Use Only

Preparer's signature ▶		Date	Check if self-employed ☐	Preparer's SSN or PTIN
Firm's name (or yours if self-employed), address, and ZIP code ▶			EIN	
			Phone no.	

410002 11-03-04

23

How To Turn Your Poker Playing Into A Business

Example 1:

SCHEDULES A&B
(Form 1040)

Department of the Treasury
Internal Revenue Service (99)

Name(s) shown on Form 1040

Schedule A - Itemized Deductions
(Schedule B is on page 2)

▶ Attach to Form 1040.   ▶ See Instructions for Schedules A and B (Form 1040).

OMB No. 1545-0074

Attachment
Sequence No. **07**

Your social security number

BEN SMITH   007 : 07 : 0007

Medical **and** **Dental** **Expenses**	**Caution.** Do not include expenses reimbursed or paid by others.				
	1	Medical and dental expenses (see page A-2)	1		
	2	Enter amount from Form 1040, line 37 [2]			
	3	Multiply line 2 by 7.5% (.075)	3		
	4	Subtract line 3 from line 1. If line 3 is more than line 1, enter -0-		4	
Taxes You **Paid** (See page A-2.)	5	State and local (check only one box): a [X] Income taxes, or b [ ] General sales taxes (see page A-2)	5	2,000.	
	6	Real estate taxes (see page A-3)	6		
	7	Personal property taxes	7		
	8	Other taxes. List type and amount ▶ _____			
		_____	8		
	9	Add lines 5 through 8		9	2,000.
Interest **You Paid** (See page A-3.) **Note:** Personal interest is not deductible.	10	Home mortgage interest and points reported to you on Form 1098	10		
	11	Home mortgage interest not reported to you on Form 1098. If paid to the person from whom you bought the home, see page A-4 and show that person's name, identifying no., and address ▶ _____			
		_____	11		
	12	Points not reported to you on Form 1098. See page A-4 for special rules	12		
	13	Investment interest. Attach Form 4952 if required. (See page A-4.)	13		
	14	Add lines 10 through 13		14	
Gifts to **Charity** If you made a gift and got a benefit for it, see page A-4.	15	Gifts by cash or check. If you made any gift of $250 or more, see page A-4	15		
	16	Other than by cash or check. If any gift of $250 or more, see page A-4. You **must** attach Form 8283 if over $500	16		
	17	Carryover from prior year	17		
	18	Add lines 15 through 17		18	
Casualty and Theft Losses	19	Casualty or theft loss(es). Attach Form 4684. (See page A-5.)		19	
Job Expenses **and Most** **Other** **Miscellaneous** **Deductions** (See page A-5.)	20	Unreimbursed employee expenses - job travel, union dues, job education, etc. Attach Form 2106 or 2106-EZ if required. (See page A-6.) ▶ _____			
		_____	20		
	21	Tax preparation fees	21		
	22	Other expenses - investment, safe deposit box, etc. List type and amount ▶ _____			
		_____			
		_____	22		
	23	Add lines 20 through 22	23		
	24	Enter amount from Form 1040, line 37 [24]			
	25	Multiply line 24 by 2% (.02)	25		
	26	Subtract line 25 from line 23. If line 25 is more than line 23, enter -0-		26	
Other **Miscellaneous** **Deductions**	27	Other - from list on page A-6. List type and amount ▶ _____			
		_____			
		_____		27	
Total **Itemized** **Deductions**	28	Is Form 1040, line 37, over $142,700 (over $71,350 if married filing separately)? [X] **No.** Your deduction is not limited. Add the amounts in the far right column for lines 4 through 27. Also, enter this amount on Form 1040, line 39. [ ] **Yes.** Your deduction may be limited. See page A-6 for the amount to enter.	▶	28	2,000.

419501 12-30-04   LHA   For Paperwork Reduction Act Notice, see Form 1040 instructions.   Schedule A (Form 1040)

EXAMPLE 1 – NOTES ON TAX RETURN

Ben shows all of his winnings on the Other Income line with a description. This is added to his W2 Wage amount for a total adjusted gross income of $63,000. See the Schedule A. He doesn't want to itemize because all he can take is the state tax withheld of $2,000 and the gambling losses of $2,500 for a total of $4,500. As you can see from the example, the Standard Deduction amount that the IRS gives you this particular year is $5,000. Since this is more than the Itemized amount, Ben needs to use this number on his return.

> **NOTE: Ben cannot add the Vegas trip expense to his gambling loss amount because his gambling is not considered a business so expenses cannot be deducted.**

Ben is allowed to deduct one exemption for himself of $3,200 which brings his taxable income to $54,800. The tax on the income for this particular year is $10,444. He had $10,000 withheld on his W2 toward his Federal tax so therefore he owes the IRS $444.

EXAMPLE 2

Let's use the same information in Example 1 but this time, instead of using gambling losses of $2,500, Ben has gambling losses of $15,000.

Example 2:

Form **1040**		U.S. Individual Income Tax Return				(99)	IRS Use Only - Do not write or staple in this space.		OMB No. 1545-0074

For the year Jan. 1-Dec. 31, 2004, or other tax year beginning _____ , 2004, ending _____ , 20 ___

Label
(See instructions on page 16.)
Use the IRS label. Otherwise, please print or type.

L
A
B
E
L

H
E
R
E

Your first name and initial	Last name	Your social security number
BEN	SMITH	007 07 0007

If a joint return, spouse's first name and initial	Last name	Spouse's social security number

Home address (number and street). If you have a P.O. box, see page 16. **Apt. no.**
99955 HEART CLUB DRIVE

▲ **Important!** ▲
You **must** enter your SSN(s) above.

City, town or post office, state, and ZIP code. If you have a foreign address, see page 16.
DIAMOND, GA 77733

Presidential Election Campaign
(See page 16.)
Note. Checking "Yes" will not change your tax or reduce your refund.
Do you, or your spouse if filing a joint return, want $3 to go to this fund? ▶

You: Yes ☐ No ☒   Spouse: Yes ☐ No ☐

Filing Status
Check only one box.

1 ☒ Single
2 ☐ Married filing jointly (even if only one had income)
3 ☐ Married filing separately. Enter spouse's SSN above and full name here. ▶
4 ☐ Head of household (with qualifying person). (See page 17.) If the qualifying person is a child but not your dependent, enter this child's name here. ▶
5 ☐ Qualifying widow(er) with dependent child (see page 17)

Exemptions

6a ☒ **Yourself.** If someone can claim you as a dependent, **do not** check box 6a ....
b ☐ Spouse

Boxes checked on 6a and 6b   **1**

c Dependents:

(1) First name Last name	(2) Dependent's social security number	(3) Dependent's relationship to you	(4) ✓ if qualifying child for child tax credit (see page 18)

No. of children on 6c who:
● lived with you
● did not live with you due to divorce or separation (see page 18)
Dependents on 6c not entered above

If more than four dependents, see page 18.

d Total number of exemptions claimed ....

Add numbers on lines above ▶ **1**

Income

Attach Form(s) W-2 here. Also attach Forms W-2G and 1099-R if tax was withheld.

If you did not get a W-2, see page 19.

Enclose, but do not attach, any payment. Also, please use Form 1040-V.

7	Wages, salaries, tips, etc. Attach Form(s) W-2	7	50,000.
8a	Taxable interest. Attach Schedule B if required	8a	
b	Tax-exempt interest. Do not include on line 8a	8b		
9a	Ordinary dividends. Attach Schedule B if required	9a	
b	Qualified dividends (see page 20)	9b		
10	Taxable refunds, credits, or offsets of state and local income taxes	10	
11	Alimony received	11	
12	Business income or (loss). Attach Schedule C or C-EZ	12	
13	Capital gain or (loss). Attach Schedule D if required. If not required, check here ▶ ☐	13	
14	Other gains or (losses). Attach Form 4797	14	
15a	IRA distributions 15a	b Taxable amount (see page 22)	15b	
16a	Pensions and annuities 16a	b Taxable amount (see page 22)	16b	
17	Rental real estate, royalties, partnerships, S corporations, trusts, etc. Attach Schedule E	17	
18	Farm income or (loss). Attach Schedule F	18	
19	Unemployment compensation	19	
20a	Social security benefits 20a	b Taxable amount (see page 24)	20b	
21	Other income. List type and amount (see page 24) GAMBLING WINNINGS 13,000.	21	13,000.
22	Add the amounts in the far right column for lines 7 through 21. This is your **total income** ▶	22	63,000.

Adjusted Gross Income

23	Educator expenses (see page 26)	23	
24	Certain business expenses of reservists, performing artists, and fee-basis government officials. Attach Form 2106 or 2106-EZ	24	
25	IRA deduction (see page 26)	25	
26	Student loan interest deduction (see page 28)	26	
27	Tuition and fees deduction (see page 29)	27	
28	Health savings account deduction. Attach Form 8889	28	
29	Moving expenses. Attach Form 3903	29	
30	One-half of self-employment tax. Attach Schedule SE	30	
31	Self-employed health insurance deduction (see page 30)	31	
32	Self-employed SEP, SIMPLE, and qualified plans	32	
33	Penalty on early withdrawal of savings	33	
34a	Alimony paid b Recipient's SSN ▶	34a	
35	Add lines 23 through 34a	35	
36	Subtract line 35 from line 22. This is your **adjusted gross income** ▶	36	63,000.

410001
11-03-04

LHA For Disclosure, Privacy Act, and Paperwork Reduction Act Notice, see page 75.

Form **1040**

Example 2:

Form 1040	BEN SMITH					007-07-0007			Page **2**

Tax and Credits

Standard Deduction for -

● People who checked any box on line 38a or 38b **Of** who can be claimed as a dependent.

● All others:

Single or Married filing separately, $4,850

Married filing jointly or Qualifying widow(er), $9,700

Head of household, $7,150

37	Amount from line 36 (adjusted gross income)			37	63,000.
38a	Check if: ☐ You were born before January 2, 1940, ☐ Blind. ☐ Spouse was born before January 2, 1940, ☐ Blind. Total boxes checked ▶ 38a				
b	If your spouse itemizes on a separate return or you were a dual-status alien, see page 31 and check here ▶ 38b ☐				
39	**Itemized deductions** (from Schedule A) **or** your **standard deduction** (see left margin)			39	15,000.
40	Subtract line 39 from line 37			40	48,000.
41	If line 37 is $107,025 or less, multiply $3,100 by the total number of exemptions claimed on line 6d. If line 37 is over $107,025, see the worksheet on page 33			41	3,200.
42	**Taxable income.** Subtract line 41 from line 40. If line 41 is more than line 40, enter -0-			42	44,800.
43	**Tax.** Check if any tax is from: **a** ☐ Form(s) 8814 **b** ☐ Form 4972			43	7,944.
44	**Alternative minimum tax.** Attach Form 6251			44	
45	Add lines 43 and 44 ▶			45	7,944.
46	Foreign tax credit. Attach Form 1116 if required		46		
47	Credit for child and dependent care expenses. Attach Form 2441		47		
48	Credit for the elderly or the disabled. Attach Schedule R		48		
49	Education credits. Attach Form 8863		49		
50	Retirement savings contributions credit. Attach Form 8880		50		
51	Child tax credit (see page 37)		51		
52	Adoption credit. Attach Form 8839		52		
53	Credits from: **a** ☐ Form 8396 **b** ☐ Form 8859		53		
54	Other credits. Check applicable box(es): **a** ☐ Form 3800 **b** ☐ Form 8801 **c** ☐ Specify		54		
55	Add lines 46 through 54. These are your **total credits**			55	
56	Subtract line 55 from line 45. If line 55 is more than line 45, enter -0- ▶			56	7,944.

Other Taxes

57	Self-employment tax. Attach Schedule SE			57	
58	Social security and Medicare tax on tip income not reported to employer. Attach Form 4137			58	
59	Additional tax on IRAs, other qualified retirement plans, etc. Attach Form 5329 if required			59	
60	Advance earned income credit payments from Form(s) W-2			60	
61	Household employment taxes. Attach Schedule H			61	
62	Add lines 56 through 61. This is your **total tax** ▶			62	7,944.

Payments

If you have a qualifying child, attach Schedule EIC.

63	Federal income tax withheld from Forms W-2 and 1099		63	10,000.	
64	2004 estimated tax payments and amount applied from 2003 return		64		
65a	**Earned income credit (EIC)**		65a		
b	Nontaxable combat pay election ▶ 65b				
66	Excess social security and tier 1 RRTA tax withheld (see page 54)		66		
67	Additional child tax credit. Attach Form 8812		67		
68	Amount paid with request for extension to file (see page 54)		68		
69	Other payments from: **a** ☐ Form 2439 **b** ☐ Form 4136 **c** ☐ Form 8885		69		
70	Add lines 63, 64, 65a, and 66 through 69. These are your **total payments** ▶			70	10,000.

Refund

Direct deposit? See page 54 and fill in 72b, 72c, and 72d.

71	If line 70 is more than line 62, subtract line 62 from line 70. This is the amount you **overpaid**			71	2,056.
72a	Amount of line 71 you want **refunded to you** ▶			72a	2,056.
b	Routing number ☐ ▶ **c** Type: ☐ Checking ☐ Savings ▶ **d** Account number ☐				
73	Amount of line 71 you want **applied to your 2005 estimated tax** ▶		73		

Amount You Owe

74	**Amount you owe.** Subtract line 70 from line 62. For details on how to pay, see page 55 ▶			74	
75	Estimated tax penalty (see page 55)		75		

Third Party Designee

Do you want to allow another person to discuss this return with the IRS (see page 56)? ☐ Yes. Complete the following. ☐ No

Designee's name ▶ ___ Phone no. ▶ ___ Personal identification number (PIN) ▶ ___

Sign Here

Joint return? See page 17. Keep a copy for your records.

Under penalties of perjury, I declare that I have examined this return and accompanying schedules and statements, and to the best of my knowledge and belief, they are true, correct, and complete. Declaration of preparer (other than taxpayer) is based on all information of which preparer has any knowledge.

Your signature	Date	Your occupation	Daytime phone number
Spouse's signature. If a joint return, **both** must sign.	Date	Spouse's occupation	

Paid Preparer's Use Only

410002 11-03-04

Preparer's signature ▶		Date	Check if self-employed ☐	Preparer's SSN or PTIN
Firm's name (or yours if self-employed), address, and ZIP code ▶			EIN	
			Phone no.	

How To Turn Your Poker Playing Into A Business

Example 2:

SCHEDULES A&B (Form 1040) Department of the Treasury Internal Revenue Service (99) Name(s) shown on Form 1040	**Schedule A - Itemized Deductions** (Schedule B is on page 2) ► Attach to Form 1040. ► See Instructions for Schedules A and B (Form 1040).	OMB No. 1545-0074 Attachment Sequence No. 07 Your social security number

BEN SMITH   007 07 0007

Medical and Dental Expenses	Caution. Do not include expenses reimbursed or paid by others.		
	1 Medical and dental expenses (see page A-2)	1	
	2 Enter amount from Form 1040, line 37 ... 2		
	3 Multiply line 2 by 7.5% (.075)	3	
	4 Subtract line 3 from line 1. If line 3 is more than line 1, enter -0-		4
Taxes You Paid (See page A-2.)	5 State and local (check only one box): a [X] Income taxes, or b [ ] General sales taxes (see page A-2)	5	2,000.
	6 Real estate taxes (see page A-3)	6	
	7 Personal property taxes	7	
	8 Other taxes. List type and amount ►	8	
	9 Add lines 5 through 8		9 2,000.
Interest You Paid (See page A-3.) Note: Personal interest is not deductible.	10 Home mortgage interest and points reported to you on Form 1098	10	
	11 Home mortgage interest not reported to you on Form 1098... ►	11	
	12 Points not reported to you on Form 1098. See page A-4 for special rules	12	
	13 Investment interest. Attach Form 4952 if required. (See page A-4.)	13	
	14 Add lines 10 through 13		14
Gifts to Charity If you made a gift and got a benefit for it, see page A-4.	15 Gifts by cash or check. If you made any gift of $250 or more, see page A-4	15	
	16 Other than by cash or check. If any gift of $250 or more, see page A-4. You **must** attach Form 8283 if over $500	16	
	17 Carryover from prior year	17	
	18 Add lines 15 through 17		18
Casualty and Theft Losses	19 Casualty or theft loss(es). Attach Form 4684. (See page A-5.)		19
Job Expenses and Most Other Miscellaneous Deductions (See page A-5.)	20 Unreimbursed employee expenses - job travel, union dues, job education, etc. Attach Form 2106 or 2106-EZ if required. (See page A-6.) ►	20	
	21 Tax preparation fees	21	
	22 Other expenses - investment, safe deposit box, etc. List type and amount ►	22	
	23 Add lines 20 through 22	23	
	24 Enter amount from Form 1040, line 37 ... 24		
	25 Multiply line 24 by 2% (.02)	25	
	26 Subtract line 25 from line 23. If line 25 is more than line 23, enter -0-		26
Other Miscellaneous Deductions	27 Other - from list on page A-6. List type and amount ►Gambling losses _____ 13,000.		27 13,000.
Total Itemized Deductions	28 Is Form 1040, line 37, over $142,700 (over $71,350 if married filing separately)? [X] No. Your deduction is not limited. Add the amounts in the far right column for lines 4 through 27. Also, enter this amount on Form 1040, line 39. ► [ ] Yes. Your deduction may be limited. See page A-6 for the amount to enter.	28	15,000.

419501 12-30-04 LHA For Paperwork Reduction Act Notice, see Form 1040 instructions.   Schedule A (Form 1040)

EXAMPLE 2 – NOTES ON TAX RETURN

Again, the adjusted gross income is the same amount of $63,000. Let's look at the Schedule A. He can now take the state withholding that was on his W2 of $2,000. Even though he had gambling losses of $15,000, he can only take $13,000 which is the amount of his gambling winnings taken on page 1 of his Form 1040, on the Other Income line. His exemption amount is the same of $3,200 which brings his taxable income to $44,800. The tax on his income for this particular year is now $7,944. He had $10,000 withheld on his W2 toward his Federal tax so therefore he receives a refund of $2,056.

EXAMPLE 3

Now, let's use the same information in Example 1 but change a few things. Ben has the same W2 and the same gambling income of $13,000 but now has gambling losses of $2,500.

Ben has a house now and he has $500 in cash contributions, mortgage interest of $5,000 and real estate taxes of $1,000 that he paid during the year. Now let's see how his return changed.

How To Turn Your Poker Playing Into A Business

Example 3:

Form **1040**	U.S. Individual Income Tax Return	(99)	IRS Use Only - Do not write or staple in this space.

For the year Jan. 1-Dec. 31,   , or other tax year beginning , ending , 20   OMB No. 1545-0074

Label
(See instructions on page 16.)

Use the IRS label. Otherwise, please print or type.

Your first name and initial	Last name	Your social security number
BEN	SMITH	007 07 0007
If a joint return, spouse's first name and initial	Last name	Spouse's social security number

Home address (number and street). If you have a P.O. box, see page 16.   Apt. no.
99955 HEART CLUB DRIVE

▲ Important! ▲
You **must** enter your SSN(s) above.

City, town or post office, state, and ZIP code. If you have a foreign address, see page 16.
DIAMOND, GA 77733

Presidential Election Campaign
(See page 16.)
Note. Checking "Yes" will not change your tax or reduce your refund.
Do you, or your spouse if filing a joint return, want $3 to go to this fund? ►   You: Yes ☐ No ☒   Spouse: Yes ☐ No ☐

Filing Status
Check only one box.

1 ☒ Single
2 ☐ Married filing jointly (even if only one had income)
3 ☐ Married filing separately. Enter spouse's SSN above and full name here. ►
4 ☐ Head of household (with qualifying person). (See page 17.) If the qualifying person is a child but not your dependent, enter this child's name here. ►
5 ☐ Qualifying widow(er) with dependent child (see page 17)

Exemptions

6a ☒ Yourself. If someone can claim you as a dependent, **do not** check box 6a
b ☐ Spouse

c Dependents: (1) First name Last name	(2) Dependent's social security number	(3) Dependent's relationship to you	(4) ✓ if qualifying child for child tax credit (see page 18)

Boxes checked on 6a and 6b: **1**
No. of children on 6c who:
• lived with you
• did not live with you due to divorce or separation (see page 18)
Dependents on 6c not entered above

If more than four dependents, see page 18.

d Total number of exemptions claimed   Add numbers on lines above ► **1**

Income

Attach Form(s) W-2 here. Also attach Forms W-2G and 1099-R if tax was withheld.

If you did not get a W-2, see page 19.

Enclose, but do not attach, any payment. Also, please use Form 1040-V.

7	Wages, salaries, tips, etc. Attach Form(s) W-2	7	50,000.
8a	Taxable interest. Attach Schedule B if required	8a	
b	Tax-exempt interest. Do not include on line 8a 8b		
9a	Ordinary dividends. Attach Schedule B if required	9a	
b	Qualified dividends (see page 20) 9b		
10	Taxable refunds, credits, or offsets of state and local income taxes	10	
11	Alimony received	11	
12	Business income or (loss). Attach Schedule C or C-EZ	12	
13	Capital gain or (loss). Attach Schedule D if required. If not required, check here ► ☐	13	
14	Other gains or (losses). Attach Form 4797	14	
15a	IRA distributions 15a b Taxable amount (see page 22)	15b	
16a	Pensions and annuities 16a b Taxable amount (see page 22)	16b	
17	Rental real estate, royalties, partnerships, S corporations, trusts, etc. Attach Schedule E	17	
18	Farm income or (loss). Attach Schedule F	18	
19	Unemployment compensation	19	
20a	Social security benefits 20a b Taxable amount (see page 24)	20b	
21	Other income. List type and amount (see page 24) GAMBLING WINNINGS 13,000.	21	13,000.
22	Add the amounts in the far right column for lines 7 through 21. This is your **total income** ►	22	63,000.

Adjusted Gross Income

23	Educator expenses (see page 26)	23	
24	Certain business expenses of reservists, performing artists, and fee-basis government officials. Attach Form 2106 or 2106-EZ	24	
25	IRA deduction (see page 26)	25	
26	Student loan interest deduction (see page 28)	26	
27	Tuition and fees deduction (see page 29)	27	
28	Health savings account deduction. Attach Form 8889	28	
29	Moving expenses. Attach Form 3903	29	
30	One-half of self-employment tax. Attach Schedule SE	30	
31	Self-employed health insurance deduction (see page 30)	31	
32	Self-employed SEP, SIMPLE, and qualified plans	32	
33	Penalty on early withdrawal of savings	33	
34a	Alimony paid b Recipient's SSN ► 34a		
35	Add lines 23 through 34a	35	
36	Subtract line 35 from line 22. This is your **adjusted gross income** ►	36	63,000.

410001 11-03-04

LHA **For Disclosure, Privacy Act, and Paperwork Reduction Act Notice, see page 75.**   Form **1040**

Example 3:

Form 1040		BEN SMITH		007-07-0007			Page 2
Tax and Credits	37	Amount from line 36 (adjusted gross income)				37	63,000.
Standard Deduction for -	38a	Check if: { You were born before January 2, 1940, Blind. } Total boxes { Spouse was born before January 2, 1940, Blind. } checked ▶ 38a					
● People who checked any box on line 38a or 38b **or** who can be claimed as a dependent.	b	If your spouse itemizes on a separate return or you were a dual-status alien, see page 31 and check here ▶ 38b					
	39	**Itemized deductions** (from Schedule A) or your **standard deduction** (see left margin)				39	11,000.
	40	Subtract line 39 from line 37				40	52,000.
	41	If line 37 is $107,025 or less, multiply $3,100 by the total number of exemptions claimed on line 6d. If line 37 is over $107,025, see the worksheet on page 33				41	3,200.
	42	**Taxable income.** Subtract line 41 from line 40. If line 41 is more than line 40, enter -0-				42	48,800.
● All others:	43	**Tax.** Check if any tax is from: a Form(s) 8814 b Form 4972				43	8,944.
Single or Married filing separately, $4,850	44	**Alternative minimum tax.** Attach Form 6251				44	
	45	Add lines 43 and 44			▶	45	8,944.
Married filing jointly or Qualifying widow(er), $9,700	46	Foreign tax credit. Attach Form 1116 if required	46				
	47	Credit for child and dependent care expenses. Attach Form 2441	47				
	48	Credit for the elderly or the disabled. Attach Schedule R	48				
Head of household, $7,150	49	Education credits. Attach Form 8863	49				
	50	Retirement savings contributions credit. Attach Form 8880	50				
	51	Child tax credit (see page 37)	51				
	52	Adoption credit. Attach Form 8839	52				
	53	Credits from: a Form 8396 b Form 8859	53				
	54	Other credits. Check applicable box(es): a Form 3800 b Form 8801 c Specify	54				
	55	Add lines 46 through 54. These are your **total credits**				55	
	56	Subtract line 55 from line 45. If line 55 is more than line 45, enter -0-			▶	56	8,944.
Other Taxes	57	Self-employment tax. Attach Schedule SE				57	
	58	Social security and Medicare tax on tip income not reported to employer. Attach Form 4137				58	
	59	Additional tax on IRAs, other qualified retirement plans, etc. Attach Form 5329 if required				59	
	60	Advance earned income credit payments from Form(s) W-2				60	
	61	Household employment taxes. Attach Schedule H				61	
	62	Add lines 56 through 61. This is your **total tax**			▶	62	8,944.
Payments	63	Federal income tax withheld from Forms W-2 and 1099	63	10,000.			
	64	2004 estimated tax payments and amount applied from 2003 return	64				
If you have a qualifying child, attach Schedule EIC.	65a	**Earned income credit (EIC)**	65a				
	b	Nontaxable combat pay election ▶	65b				
	66	Excess social security and tier 1 RRTA tax withheld (see page 54)	66				
	67	Additional child tax credit. Attach Form 8812	67				
	68	Amount paid with request for extension to file (see page 54)	68				
	69	Other payments from: a Form 2439 b Form 4136 c Form 8885	69				
	70	Add lines 63, 64, 65a, and 66 through 69. These are your **total payments**			▶	70	10,000.
Refund	71	If line 70 is more than line 62, subtract line 62 from line 70. This is the amount you **overpaid**				71	1,056.
Direct deposit? See page 54 and fill in 72b, 72c, and 72d.	72a	Amount of line 71 you want **refunded to you**			▶	72a	1,056.
	b	Routing number ▶ c Type: Checking Savings ▶ d Account number					
	73	Amount of line 71 you want **applied to your 2005 estimated tax** ▶	73				
Amount You Owe	74	**Amount you owe.** Subtract line 70 from line 62. For details on how to pay, see page 55			▶	74	
	75	Estimated tax penalty (see page 55)	75				
Third Party Designee		Do you want to allow another person to discuss this return with the IRS (see page 56)? Yes. Complete the following. No					
		Designee's name Phone no. Personal identification number (PIN)					
Sign Here Joint return? See page 17. Keep a copy for your records.		Under penalties of perjury, I declare that I have examined this return and accompanying schedules and statements, and to the best of my knowledge and belief, they are true, correct, and complete. Declaration of preparer (other than taxpayer) is based on all information of which preparer has any knowledge.					
		Your signature Date Your occupation Daytime phone number					
		Spouse's signature. If a joint return, **both** must sign. Date Spouse's occupation					
Paid Preparer's Use Only		Preparer's signature ▶ Date Check if self-employed Preparer's SSN or PTIN					
410002 11-03-04		Firm's name (or yours if self-employed), address, and ZIP code ▶ EIN Phone no.					

How To Turn Your Poker Playing Into A Business

Example 3:

SCHEDULES A&B (Form 1040)	Schedule A - Itemized Deductions	OMB No. 1545-0074

Department of the Treasury
Internal Revenue Service (99)

(Schedule B is on page 2)

▶ Attach to Form 1040.   ▶ See Instructions for Schedules A and B (Form 1040).

Attachment Sequence No. **07**

Name(s) shown on Form 1040

Your social security number

BEN SMITH   007 : 07 : 0007

Medical and Dental Expenses		Caution. Do not include expenses reimbursed or paid by others.			
	1	Medical and dental expenses (see page A-2)	1		
	2	Enter amount from Form 1040, line 37	2		
	3	Multiply line 2 by 7.5% (.075)	3		
	4	Subtract line 3 from line 1. If line 3 is more than line 1, enter -0-		4	
Taxes You Paid (See page A-2.)	5	State and local (check only one box): a [X] Income taxes, or b [ ] General sales taxes (see page A-2)	5	2,000.	
	6	Real estate taxes (see page A-3)	6	1,000.	
	7	Personal property taxes	7		
	8	Other taxes. List type and amount ▶ _____	8		
	9	Add lines 5 through 8		9	3,000.
Interest You Paid (See page A-3.)	10	Home mortgage interest and points reported to you on Form 1098	10	5,000.	
	11	Home mortgage interest not reported to you on Form 1098. If paid to the person from whom you bought the home, see page A-4 and show that person's name, identifying no., and address ▶ _____	11		
Note: Personal interest is not deductible.	12	Points not reported to you on Form 1098. See page A-4 for special rules	12		
	13	Investment interest. Attach Form 4952 if required. (See page A-4.)	13		
	14	Add lines 10 through 13		14	5,000.
Gifts to Charity If you made a gift and got a benefit for it, see page A-4.	15	Gifts by cash or check. If you made any gift of $250 or more, see page A-4	15	500.	
	16	Other than by cash or check. If any gift of $250 or more, see page A-4. You **must** attach Form 8283 if over $500	16		
	17	Carryover from prior year	17		
	18	Add lines 15 through 17		18	500.
Casualty and Theft Losses	19	Casualty or theft loss(es). Attach Form 4684. (See page A-5.)		19	
Job Expenses and Most Other Miscellaneous Deductions (See page A-5.)	20	Unreimbursed employee expenses - job travel, union dues, job education, etc. Attach Form 2106 or 2106-EZ if required. (See page A-6.) ▶ _____	20		
	21	Tax preparation fees	21		
	22	Other expenses - investment, safe deposit box, etc. List type and amount ▶ _____	22		
	23	Add lines 20 through 22	23		
	24	Enter amount from Form 1040, line 37	24		
	25	Multiply line 24 by 2% (.02)	25		
	26	Subtract line 25 from line 23. If line 25 is more than line 23, enter -0-		26	
Other Miscellaneous Deductions	27	Other - from list on page A-6. List type and amount ▶Gambling losses _____ 2,500. _____		27	2,500.
Total Itemized Deductions	28	Is Form 1040, line 37, over $142,700 (over $71,350 if married filing separately)? [X] **No.** Your deduction is not limited. Add the amounts in the far right column for lines 4 through 27. Also, enter this amount on Form 1040, line 39. [ ] **Yes.** Your deduction may be limited. See page A-6 for the amount to enter.		28	11,000.

419501 12-30-04   LHA   **For Paperwork Reduction Act Notice, see Form 1040 instructions.**   Schedule A (Form 1040)

EXAMPLE 3 – NOTES ON TAX RETURN

Again, the adjusted gross income is the same amount of $63,000. Let's look at the Schedule A. He can take the state withholding that was on his W2 of $2,000. He can also take the real estate taxes of $1,000, the mortgage interest of $5,000, the charitable contributions of $500 and the gambling losses of $2,500. This gives Ben a total of $11,000 for itemized deductions. His exemption amount is the same of $3,200 which brings his taxable income to $48,800. The tax on his income for this particular year is now $8,944. He had $10,000 withheld on his W2 toward his Federal tax so therefore he receives a refund of $1,056.

Hopefully these examples will give you a good idea at how important it is to keep up with expenses. If you do not have records of your expenses, you lose out on a large amount as a tax deduction. This could mean the difference between owing the IRS and getting a refund.

IMPORTANT: Remember that the standard deduction amount and exemption amount changes every year. Please refer to the IRS website for the current year's figures.

I have spoken with many people that have a "real" job but they also play tournaments all over the United States. They are receiving Form W2G and want my advice on what to do. Again, you are required to list all of your income on the front page and your losses on the Schedule A. I feel that if you are playing enough to win a tournament, you probably have more in winnings than what is on your Form W2G. Be sure you put all of the winnings down in addition to the amount on the Form. It would seem very odd that the amount on the Form is all that you have won for the year! But I cannot stress enough for you to keep up with receipts or keep the log that is in Chapter 8 so you can substantiate your wagers to the IRS if necessary.

SHOW ME THE MONEY!
(POKER AS A BUSINESS)

♠ ♥ ♣ ♦

My client and I met before April 15th to prepare his taxes. We started discussing our favorite subject of poker and he asked if I was playing.

"Are you kidding? I am stuck here until tax season is over. What about you?"

"I haven't played in a while but a buddy of mine has been playing on the internet a lot. In fact", he said, "he has decided to play poker full-time."

"Really," I replied, "I hope he is getting started on the right foot."

"He really could use some advice because he has decided to go full force with it and is even having home games."

"Well there are a lot of deductions that he needs to keep up with to offset his business income." I said.

So, you have determined that your poker play falls under the rules of being a business. As a professional poker player, how do you make sure that you start off on the right foot and are meeting the criteria to have legitimate expenses that can be deductible?

There are a few things that you will want to do. Here is a brief checklist:

- Open a business checking account
- Obtain a business license or permit
- Print business cards/letterhead/envelopes
- Have an office address or Post Office box
- Obtain any necessary insurance – i.e. liability/health, etc.
- File with the state (if necessary)
- Decide on recordkeeping procedures
- Consult an accountant
- Consult an attorney (if necessary)
- Decide on a business plan

The above items are a few of the ways to begin a business. Some may not apply, depending on your situation.

One very important item is to open a business checking account. This way you can deposit winnings and write out expenses from the account. It is also good if you can have a credit card that you strictly use for your business. The more that you keep this separated from non-business transactions, the better you will be.

Business cards are a great tool for your business. You can use it to promote yourself or your services such as a prop or shill player or even to give poker lessons.

Insurance may be a good idea for liability purposes. Some people just want to sue you for the craziest things so it wouldn't be a bad idea to check with a local insurance carrier. Also, look into health insurance which is deductible.

If you have assets, such as a computer/fax/copier/etc., you may want business property insurance.

Recordkeeping is very important and is discussed in more detail in Chapter 8. When you start your business, make sure you figure out the best and easiest way to keep up with your activity for the year. This is truly a large key to your success and is necessary in tax compliance.

Your best bet in your new endeavor is to consult a professional such as an accountant and/or an attorney. They will be able to advise you on your unique situation so you can start planning as early as possible. Knowing what to do ahead of time will save you trouble and frustration later on down the road.

As a professional gambler, you report your gambling activity on a Schedule C, Profit and Loss from Business. This form goes along with your personal tax return (Form 1040) and submitted to the government. This is the form where you summarize what you made from gambling, what money you lost, and the gambling-related expenses that you had.

At this time, the IRS will not allow you to deduct more expenses than income – even if you are considered a business. Of course this is not true for other types of businesses. "Regular" businesses can take more expenses than income and have losses on their tax return.

Gambling is totally different from other businesses. It has always been the rule that if you have gambling income you can offset it with gambling losses. This rule applies to the "hobby" gambler that can only offset these winnings if they can itemize. (For information on itemizing, see Chapter 3). By taking it a step further and becoming a business, the IRS still applies the gambling rules. Basically, you cannot exceed gambling winnings and you have to show a net profit of zero even if your expenses are more than your income.

In many cases, taxpayers have attempted to take their gambling losses on a Schedule C that were more than the gambling income. This has been challenged over and over and still the IRS has only allowed losses up to the amount of income. Their argument is that even through IRS Code Section 162(a) allows deductions for a trade or business expense, code Section 165(d) prohibits taxpayers from deducting wagering losses, except to the extent of wagering gains. You cannot claim a net loss. Professional gamblers have challenged these rules and constantly lose against the IRS in court.

My opinion is that this will be challenged until one day a) the taxpayer will win or b) it will cause the IRS to change their rule. Too many people are becoming professional gamblers (mostly due to the poker phenomena) and the IRS should not be able to label gambling as the red-headed stepchild. The distinction of gambling as a reputable business may take a period of time but I feel that day will come.

So what are the tax benefits of treating your gambling as a business? Well, it's the only way to take your gambling-related expenses even if you can only net them to zero. If you had income and were a hobby, you would still have to claim the income on the front page of your tax return. Remember the expenses are not deductible if you are a hobby, only the losses up to the income amount and only if you can itemize. Therefore, the adjusted gross income for a professional gambler would be lower than the hobby gambler. (See Glossary for detail of terms).

There are credits that you may be able to take that are based on the amount of your adjusted gross income (AGI). The lower your AGI is, the more likely you are to be able to take other credits or deductions. Some of these credits include Earned Income Credits, Child Tax Credits, Education Credits, deductibility amount of IRA contributions, phase-outs of personal exemptions, itemized deductions, etc. I'm sure you get the jist of what I am saying. This is the more complicated area that an accountant can help you to understand based on your particular situation.

MISSING A DEDUCTION
CAN "COST" YOU

♠ ♥ ♣ ♦

Jerome, a "Professional" poker player, sat down next to me at a casino. When he learned that I was a CPA, we began to discuss his profession. Jerome plays poker for a living. Just like any other job, he goes to work every day, be it a casino or on-line, and plays to win. He has a family to support and is counted on to pay the bills. His wife has a steady job in a casino so there is some consistency to their cash flow.

Jerome has been a professional poker player for 9 years and has never treated it as a business on his tax return. He states that he does win more than he loses and puts the money in his checking account. He hopes that he picks up all of his deposits from poker as income.

"Uh, oh," I said, "did you know that when the IRS audits you, they ask for all of your bank statements and compare the deposits to what you have claimed on your return. You better have a good *explanation if the amount of your deposits last year does not match what you reported on your tax return."*

Jerome was a little surprised at this. He stated that he had to deposit the cash in order to pay bills but hasn't necessarily kept the best records. Over the past year, Jerome now has tremendous winnings from tournaments and on-line games. He has received a Form W2G from several casinos for tournament wins. He knows that he can take deductions from expenses he has to offset his winnings. The question is what can he deduct?

Now that you have established that you are a business, what expenses can you write off? The IRS is really focused on the term "ordinary and necessary." The worse thing that you can do is be abusive in your expenses. The nature of your expenses depends on several factors. First and foremost, if you have winnings for the year of $50,000 and you spend $5,000 for a business dinner that may not be ordinary based on your income.

Now, if you just won the World Series of Poker for $5 million, $5,000 isn't necessarily that unusual! It is all relative so just be careful. What can you deduct? Here is a list of the many items that you may want to think about as the expense relates to your business:

- Accounting/Legal Fees
- Advertising/Marketing
- Automobile Expenses (see Chapter 6)
- Bank Charges
- Books
- Computer/Fax/Office Equipment
- Dues & Subscriptions
- Education/Seminars
- Furniture
- Insurance-Health/Business
- Interest Expenses
- Internet Costs
- Meals and Entertainment (see Chapter 7)
- Rent or Lease Expenses
- Software
- Supplies
- Taxes & Licenses

- Telephone/Cell Phones
- Travel Expenses (see Chapter 7)

The above expenses must be related to your gambling business. Let's discuss several of these expenses:

Accounting and Legal Fees – These are fees charged by accountants that are ordinary and necessary expenses of operating a business. This includes preparation of your Schedule C for your tax return. Legal advice concerning your business is also deductible.

Advertising/Marketing Expenses – Costs to advertise your business, including business cards or flyers, are deductible. Advertising to influence legislation is not deductible.

Bank Charges – Fees charged by your bank to maintain your business checking account or charges for any overdraft fees are fully deductible.

Books – You can deduct any books that you purchase related to your industry. These include any books to learn more about the industry, books in running a business or other educational books that relate to having a business.

Computer/Fax/Office Equipment – This includes all equipment, such as computers, printers, fax machines, copiers, etc. that are directly used in your business.

When you purchase equipment that you use in your business, you can deduct the cost. If it is a large amount, say over $1,000 you may need to depreciate it instead of taking the entire amount in the year of purchase. If you purchase an item that should be depreciated, you may be able to write the entire amount off if you have a profit in your business for the year. This is called a Section 179 deduction. Basically it means that you can take the full amount of a large expense in the year that you purchase to accelerate the deduction. There is a maximum amount of assets that you can take for Section 179 per year. This is a large amount so, again, check the IRS website for the amount, as it changes each year.

Property that you can take this Section 179 is basically machinery, equipment and furniture. You cannot use the Section 179 for real property such as buildings and structural components, including any building improvements.

Dues & Subscriptions – Dues to business organizations such as trade or professional associations, the chamber of commerce, civic clubs, and service organizations such as Rotary Clubs are deductible.

Any organization where the main purpose is to provide entertainment is not deductible. Such examples are Country Clubs, Golf or athletic dues, airport and lunch/dinner clubs.

Education/Seminars – These are seminars or education costs related to your business including registration fees for conferences. This is not to be confused with Tuition and Fee expenses, which is an entirely different animal that goes on a different part of your tax return.

Furniture – This is any furniture that you might need for your business. For example, if you are an internet player, you may need a desk and chair or a bookshelf, etc.

Insurance-Business/Health – Having your own business may mean that you want to have insurance. Deductible insurance includes casualty, credit insurance (to cover losses from unpaid debts), liability and also general business insurance, such as for your property.

Health insurance is a bit different. You can deduct up to 100% of your health insurance for yourself, spouse and children if you are self-employed. The deduction can be taken on the front page of your tax return as an adjustment to income. However, if you do not have a profit, you cannot take this deduction here. It has to go on the Form for Itemizing under Medical and is now subject to limitations (See Chapter 11). This is really a great deduction for a business that has profits. Be sure not to miss this one!

Interest Expenses – This is interest that you pay on business related debt. For instance, if you go out and get a business loan, you can deduct the interest that you pay each year on the loan.

You also can deduct the business portion of your auto loan interest that you pay if you use actual expenses. Be sure to see the Chapter 6 on Auto Expenses for a detail on this.

Interest/finance charges that you pay on credit cards can be deducted as long as the interest that you paid was for business expenses. It is important to try to keep business and personal loans/credit card charges as separate as possible. By combining these, you have to figure out how much of the interest is related to your business. This leaves room for the IRS to argue and re-allocate some of your deduction as personal.

Internet – The cost of using the internet in your business is deductible. This is especially true for people that play poker on the internet. Be sure to remember this deduction as this may add up to a substantial amount per year. Any modems or wireless fees are also deductible.

Rent/Lease – Rent that you pay for space where you conduct your business is deductible. You can also deduct rent or lease payments for equipment or machinery that you use.

Software – You can deduct the cost of the software that you use in your business, such as an accounting program that helps you keep up with income and expenses. You can also deduct the cost of any poker software that assists helps you to improve your skills.

Supplies – Supplies that you may deduct can include playing cards, chips, dice, pens, paper, calculators, folders, notepads, etc. The possibilities are numerous.

Taxes & Licenses – If you have any business related taxes, such as a personal property tax (usually imposed on the State level), it is deductible. You also can deduct the cost of a business licenses or any other licenses that you need for your business (sorry, a drivers licenses doesn't count!)

Telephone/Cell Phones – You can deduct the cost of your telephone at home if you put in a separate business line. If you do not have a separate line at home, you cannot deduct the base fee and taxes of the first line. Therefore, if you only have one phone line in the house, take your monthly bill and subtract the base rate (including taxes) and then deduct the difference. You also can deduct your business long distance phone calls and fees.

Everyone has a cell phone. As a gambler, you most likely can argue the full cost of the cellular phone bill as well as the cost of the phone. Again, the purpose needs to be business. If the majority of the use is not, you need to pro-rate the bill based on the business vs. personal use.

There are many more categories but I wanted to touch on the most popular and perhaps jog your memory on things that you haven't thought of.

> **IMPORTANT** – *Credit card charges for business expenses are deductible even though you keep a running balance on your credit card! You do not have to have your credit card paid off in order to deduct expenses. The IRS looks at the charge date and allows you to write off the expense based on when you charged the item. What this also means is that if you charge something on or before December 31st 2005, but you do not pay the charge until the middle of January, 2006 when your statement drops, this is a 2005 expense deduction.*

Office in Home Deduction

Many people have asked me about the business use of their home, also known as the office in home deduction. This is a deduction that most people cannot take if they are gamblers. The rules are strict and would most likely only relate to internet gamblers. Summarized below are the basics of the office in home deduction.

In order to qualify for the Office in Home deduction, part of your home must be used regularly and exclusively as one of the following:

1. Regularly and exclusively as the principal place of business;
2. Regularly and exclusively as the place where you meet and deal with your clients or customers in the normal course of your business, or
3. In connection with your business if you use a separate structure that is not attached to your home.

The IRS considers where most of your business activities are performed and where most of your time is spent in order to deduct expenses for the business use of your home.

As you can probably figure out, most poker players are not able to use this deduction since the majority of their business activity is in a card room or casino. However, the player that rarely goes to a casino and plays primarily on-line can possibly take advantage of this deduction.

"DETAILING" YOUR AUTO DEDUCTIONS

♠ ♥ ♣ ♦

I pulled into the Casino parking lot. Pulling up next to me was Scott, a poker pro, in his new Porsche Boxster.

"Life must be pretty good," I said with a grin.

"It is," he replied as he closed his door. "I am going to write this baby off on my taxes. In fact, a guy told me that I can put my web site on the car with a magnetic sign and write the whole thing off as advertising."

I shook my head. "Whoever is telling you that is crazy! You can write off your car but not like that! You need to make sure you understand the REAL rules as a poker pro," I said.

"How about we go for a test drive and you can straighten me out?" he laughed.

You have a car that you use for your poker playing business. You have heard 'this and that' about car deductions but what is really true?

> **NOTE: If you have your own business, and use the car in the business, your car is deductible based on the business percentage used.**

I can not begin to tell you how many people say that their car is 100% business. Can that be true? It's not too often that your car is 100% business but, as always, it depends.

Let's start with the easy stuff. Your car is deductible if it is used for business. If it is used for both personal and business, you need to figure out the percentage for each and apply that percentage to the total expenses at the end of the year.

If you use your car to go to the grocery store, it ceases to be 100% business use. Now, if you have another car that you have just for personal use, then it is easier to justify that one of your autos is all business.

Here is the bad part for someone that works out of their home but cannot use the Office in Home Deduction (See the end of Chapter 5). The IRS says that if you leave your home and go to a place of business, this is commuting mileage and is not deductible. What if you go from your house to the casino? It is considered commuting. Plain and simple.

What if you have a small office away from your home that you rent? The rules may be different since you now have a place of business. If your drive to your office and then to the casino, this mileage is considered business mileage.

What if you don't have an office and have to travel to a casino far away from your home? The IRS looks to see if you are in "business travel status". This is where your duties require you to be away from your home substantially longer than an ordinary day's work AND sleep or rest is required to meet the demands of the work. So apply this to your situation to make the business determination.

Now that you have determined how much is business mileage, how does the write-off work? There are two ways to deduct your car – Mileage and Actual. You can write off the business miles that you drive each year or you can choose to write off the actual costs of operating your car.

Standard Mileage Method
This is available for a vehicle that you own or you lease.

First, with a leased vehicle, once you decide you want to use the mileage method, you must use it for the entire lease period. You cannot switch to the actual method.

With a car that you own, the election to use the standard mileage method must generally be made in the first year the car is placed in service. Placed in service is when it is available for use in your business. In later years, you can switch to the actual expense method but then you cannot take depreciation on the car if it is considered fully depreciated.

The standard mileage method is calculated by taking the total amount of business miles that you drove during the year and multiplying it by the standard mileage rate that the IRS allows. Sounds pretty simple but sometimes the IRS changes the rate in the middle of the year!

In 2005, the rate was 40 ½ cents per mile up until 8/31/05. Then, because of the gas problems with Hurricane Katrina, the IRS raised the rate from 9/1/05 to the end of the year to be 48 ½ cents per mile. So, you had to do two different calculations with the two different rates.

The standard mileage rate is theoretically supposed to cover depreciation, insurance, gas, oil changes, tires, etc. By using the mileage method, you do not have to keep up with the actual costs of maintaining your car for business.

The items that are not covered by the mileage method that can be also be deducted are business parking fees and tolls, any property taxes that you have to pay to your state and local government, and any interest on your auto loan.

Actual Expense Method
This method limits you to the actual costs to operate your vehicle for business. Actual car expenses include:

Depreciation	Oil
Garage Rent	Parking Fees
Gas	Registration Fees
Insurance	Repairs
Lease Payments	Tires
Licenses	Tolls

Again, you can only deduct the business portion of these expenses. The easiest way is to keep up with your total miles for the year and your business miles. Then come up with a percentage of business use and multiply that percentage by the total amount of actual expenses that you have incurred.

Example: Mike uses his car for business everyday by driving to a rented office and then to the casino. He also used his car to drive to the grocery store and to the mall. He drove his car 20,000 miles for the year and drove 18,000 miles for his poker business. He can claim 90% (18,000 /20,000) of the cost of operating his car as a business expense. Therefore, he adds up all of his actual expenses for the year and multiplies it by the 90% for his business deduction amount.

The difficult part of using the actual method is taking depreciation. This is the "complicated" part of using the actual method for your car expenses. Depreciation begins when the car is placed in service.

Your car is considered a capital expense. Because the benefits last longer than a year, you generally cannot deduct a capital expense in one year. Therefore, you have to recover this cost by depreciating the cost of the auto over several years.

The way to begin is with the basis of the car. The basis in a car for figuring the depreciation is generally its cost. The method that you select to depreciate a car is usually a method called MACRS (Modified Accelerated Cost Recovery System). Generally, you must use the car more than 50% for business or you must use another method of depreciation called the straight-line method. This sounds scary, and it is a bit complicated. Cars are generally classified as 5 year property so you write off the cost, spreading it over 5 years. There is a limitation on the first year of depreciation that you can take of up to $2,960 under this method. (The

$2,960 is the amount for 2004). The amount is different each year. Again, this is reduced by your personal percentage. Unfortunately, it may take longer than 5 years to depreciation your auto, depending on how much it cost.

Now, that is about as deep as I am going to get into MACRS. Basically, this is the point where you need more help that what I can tell you in this book. Granted, you can do this yourself with one of the off-the-shelf tax return preparation programs. It will calculate the depreciation for you so you won't need to be put to sleep any further.

Here is a very basic example:
Jack bought a car in January for $20,000 and placed it in service immediately. He uses the car 75% for business. Jack has to figure the basis, or the amount of business use. In this case it is the $20,000 x 75% = $15,000. This is how you figure your business basis in the car. The difference of $5,000 is not deductible because it is personal use.

Jack can only take $2,220 of depreciation on his car in the first year. This is the $2,960 limit times his business use of 75%. The IRS has these limits on depreciation because they don't want someone to buy a $100,000 car and end up with a write off of around $60,000!

Unfortunately, there are all kinds of rules and exceptions. An off-the-shelf software program should be able to walk you through this but an accountant (preferably a CPA) will be able to actually do this calculation also. (Beware if you want them to explain it!)

But there is better news that I want up should be aware of – Accelerated Depreciation. Accelerated Depreciation is where the depreciation deduction is more than the limit of $2,960.

Accelerated Depreciation is an exception to the rules that many of you have heard of in the news lately. There is a deduction called Section 179. I touched on this in Chapter 5. This is a method to write off your car pretty fast. It's for vehicles that are usually sport utility and trucks that have a gross vehicle weight of over 6,000 pounds. This has to be primarily designed or used to carry passengers over public streets, etc. with no more than a 14,000 gross vehicle weight. As of 2004, you can write off up to $25,000 of the cost of the car and then depreciate the remainder (if any) over the 5 years.

Remember, as good as this may sound, there are some disadvantages and exceptions. You cannot use the Section 179 for more profit than you have. For example, you do your tax return and calculate that you have a profit for the year of $15,000. The car you purchased that is 100% business at the beginning of the year, cost exactly $25,000. You can only deduct $15,000 of the car – the remainder has to be depreciated. There are also some repercussions if you take the Section 179 and sell your car. Please read more detail on this in the IRS Publication 463 for your particular situation.

So, the next important thing to remember with respect to your auto deduction is to keep accurate records! Please see Chapter 8 for a great way to do this. You can also link to the website at **www.pokerdeductions.com** for a spreadsheet.

A GREAT "TEAM" – TRAVEL,
ENTERTAINMENT AND MEALS

♠ ♥ ♣ ♦

Everyone in the poker room knew Steve. And you could tell he thought he was God's gift to the world. He strutted up to my table and sat across from me in the number 7 seat. He winked at me.

Oh geez, I thought, another one of those. He was making conversation over the table with me and I tried to ignore him. He finally told the dealer that he wanted a seat change to my side of the table when the first seat came available. I immediately started chatting with the guys on each side of me, hoping that they would stay for a while. No luck. One left to go to dinner so Steve slithered his way toward me with his rack of chips.

"So, are you here alone?" he asked. "No, my girlfriend is with me and she is playing the five cent slots. She isn't a big gambler" I said with a grin.

"I would love to buy you dinner tonight", he whispered. "Gee, I

would love to but can't. We are eating at the restaurant in the hotel and, oh, look at the time, I am running late for my reservation." "I'll catch up with you later," he barked after me.

As my girlfriend and I sat in the restaurant, I turned pale when I saw Steve walking toward our table. He sat down and announced that he couldn't stay but he wanted to buy us dinner because, as a "pro", he can write off all his meals. Heck, he even writes off his strip club trips.

"Guess what, Steve", I said. "An accountant would never turn down a free meal but as far as a write off, you better watch your back with the IRS with that attitude!"

Having your own business does allow you to write off expenses such as travel, entertainment and meals. However, you really need to be careful and know what you can legally write off and what you cannot.

TRAVEL

Let's start off with travel expenses. With poker as a business, you may have to fly to casinos for tournaments in places as far away as Paris or Aruba. The IRS says that you can deduct ordinary and necessary expenses that you have when you are traveling away from home on business. They also throw in the phrase that says that the type of expense that you can deduct depends on the "facts and circumstances".

What are some of these travel expenses? Here are a few examples:

- **Transportation** – Airplane, train, bus, taxi, shuttles, etc.

- **Baggage & Shipping** – Sending baggage or sample displays

- **Car** – See Chapter 6, also the cost of a rental car is deductible for the business portion

- **Lodging and Meals** – Food, beverages, taxes, tips, hotel rooms, etc.

- **Cleaning** – Dry cleaning and laundry while you are away

- **Telephone** – Business calls while on your trip, this includes paying for the use of a fax machine or the internet

You can deduct all your travel expenses of getting to and from your business destination if your trip is entirely for business. This includes trips outside the United States.

Even if you did not spend your entire time away on a business activity, you can deduct your entire trip if at least one of these exceptions apply:

Exception 1 – No substantial control – This applies if you did not have substantial control over arranging the trip. (This most likely does not apply to your business – but there are 2 more exceptions to qualify for!)

Exception 2 – Outside the United States no more than a week – Your trip is considered entirely for business if you are outside the U.S. a week or less. This means seven consecutive days, not counting the day you leave the U.S.

Exception 3 – Less than 25% of time on personal activities – Your trip is considered entirely for business if you were outside the U.S. for more than a week and you spent less than 25% of the total time on non-business activities.

Exception 4 – Vacation was not a major consideration – Your trip is considered entirely for business if you can establish that a personal vacation was not the main reason, even if you do have substantial control over the trip.

Travel expenses for other individuals that are not related to a business purpose are not deductible. If a bona fide business purpose exists, and you can prove a real business purpose for a person's presence, you generally can deduct their expenses.

If you use a free ticket, such as using your frequent flyer points, you cannot deduct this. You can only deduct amounts that you pay for, not what it would have cost. Also remember that if you take a trip for personal reasons, you can only deduct expenses that you may incur for a business reason while you are there. You have the burden of figuring out a fair calculation.

Now, a quick note on Luxury Water Travel. If you travel by a cruise ship or other form of luxury water travel for business purposes, there is a daily limit on the amount you can deduct. It is based on the Federal per diem rate and it is twice that rate. (The Federal per diem rate is the amount paid to federal government employees for daily living expenses). For 2004, the highest Federal per diem rate was $259. Therefore for luxury water travel, the amount is $518 per day.

What if you are going on the cruise to play in a big televised poker tournament? For a 6-day cruise, you had to pay $3,500. Your deduction cannot be more than $3,108 which is the $518 times 6 days.

If meals and entertainment are separately stated on your bill, you are limited to 50% deductibility. See more of this in the section below that discusses Meals.

Conventions that you attend that benefits your trade or business are deductible. You cannot deduct the travel expenses for your family unless they are assisting you. If the particular convention is for political or investment purposes that is not related to your business, the expenses are not deductible.

ENTERTAINMENT

Business expenses that you have to entertain a client, customer or employee may be deductible. However, almost all Meals and Entertainment expenses are only 50% deductible. The IRS did this to curtail previous abuse.

The general rule is that ordinary and necessary expenses are deductible if they are directly-related or associated with your business. The IRS definition of ordinary is "one that is common and accepted in your field of business, trade or profession". Their definition of necessary is "one that is helpful and appropriate, although not necessarily required, for your business". Hmmm.

Here is the test:

To be directly-related, the entertainment had to take place in a clear business setting or the main purpose was to actively conduct business. Also, you engaged in business with the person when you were entertaining them and you had a substantial expectation of deriving income from the entertaining or some other business benefit.

To be associated, the entertaining is associated with your trade or business and it is before or after a substantial business discussion.

Other rules are that you cannot "double-dip" in deducting the meal as an entertainment expense when you are also claiming it as a travel expense. The IRS also looks at lavish or extravagant expenses under the circumstances.

What if you want to have a Skybox or another type of private luxury box? The IRS states that if you rent such for more than one event at the same sports arena, you cannot deduct more than the price of a non-luxury box seat ticket. For food and beverage in the skybox, you can deduct these subject to the limits (50% deductible). They also say it must be reasonable (a judgment call).

Now, how do you prove these expenses are business? The elements to be proven to the IRS are Amount, Time, Place, Business Purpose and/or Business Relationship. If you are audited, and you charged an entertainment expense (or meal), you need to have all of those items stated on the receipt or credit card statement. You need to be able to address those elements if audited for those expenses.

MEALS

You can deduct meals that are business related or meals that are necessary for you to perform your duties while traveling away from home for business. Again, meals and entertainment are only 50% deductible.

You can figure your meals expense one of two ways – actual cost or the standard meal allowance.

If you use the actual method, you must keep records of your actual cost and again, you must justify the Amount, Time, Place, Business Purpose and/or Business Relationship.

If you use the standard meal allowance, it allows you to use a set amount for your daily meals and incidental expenses instead of keeping records of the actual costs. The set amount varies on where and when you travel. These figures are found in the IRS Publication 1542, which is available at www.irs.gov. In 2004, the amount for most U.S. cities is

$31/day. You may be better off using the actual method! Using the standard meal allowance does not get you out of the justification of Time, Place and Business Purpose.

I recommend that you write the business purpose and who you are with on the back of the receipt at a restaurant, etc. You then should staple the receipt to a summary page or to the credit card statement to make it easer to keep up with. It is hard to re-create this information unless you keep really good records in a journal or calendar.

The 50% deductibility limit that I mentioned before relates to most Meals and Entertainment. Examples also include Taxes and tips related to a meals/entertainment, parking at a sports arena, rent paid for a room to host a dinner or cocktail party, etc. Costs to travel, such as a taxi, to a meal or entertainment facility are 100% deductible.

Exceptions to the 50% are meals provided to employees at the employer's place of business (for the employer's convenience), promotional activities made available to the general public (such as dinners provided for an investment seminar) and employee summer picnics or a holiday party. Therefore, advertising expenses are not subject to the 50% limit if you provide meals and entertainment to the general public as a means of advertising or promoting goodwill in the community. Also, you are not subject to the 50% if you pay for a package deal that includes a ticket to a qualified charitable sports event.

YOU NEED R&R
RECORDS AND RECEIPTS

♠ ♥ ♣ ♦

The internet - it is my answer to wanting to play poker but not wanting to drive 6 hours to do so. It was a cold rainy Sunday and I decided to jump on-line for a $100 one-table tournament. The pay-offs are pretty good if you place first or second.

I logged in as CPAEvil and found the tournament. As I clicked on to pay my buy-in and fee, I noticed a familiar screen name sitting to my right. Great, this guy won the trip to the Caribbean last year. Even though his screen name leads you to believe it's a girl, he is one sharp guy. I typed hello in the dialogue box since he and I have chatted before.

"Hey Evil," he said. "How's the numbers business?" "Not as fun as these numbers," I replied.

"Hey, I need your help," he said "I am having a problem keeping up with receipts to deduct all this traveling and other expenses I have incurred since turning pro."

"I hope you realize all of the things you can deduct and what kinds of records that you should be keeping," I replied. "I bet you have a few tricks I don't know about," he said. "Oh yeah," I replied "after this, e-mail me and I'll give you pointers that will have you buying me drinks in the sun."

I was just dealt pocket aces and of all people to go up against, he happened to raise me. I re-raised and he went all-in. What else could I do before the flop? I clicked "all-in" and saw his pair of kings. The flop had a 2 of Hearts a 6 of Clubs and a 3 of Clubs, the turn was a Jack of Clubs. Then it was over, a King of Hearts on the river.

"I'll wait to hear from you later, but I may be sending you my bill this time." I left the table and logged out to my glass of wine that was waiting for me.

Why keep records? There are several reasons why you should. First of all, you can monitor how your business is doing. Second, you need records to prepare an accurate tax return. **But, most importantly, you need records for proof in the event of an audit.**

If you are audited, the burden of proof is placed on the IRS, <u>provided</u> <u>that</u> you have complied with the substantiation and record-keeping requirement of the Internal Revenue Code (Section 7491). You, the taxpayer, must maintain records if you are the lucky winner of an audit.

What does this mean? If you have income or, most importantly, expenses claimed on your tax return, you need to have a very clear record of this.

How do you sit at a poker table or at an internet poker room and keep up with your winnings and losses? Because poker rooms do not monitor winnings like slot play does, there is no way to know how much you have cleared unless you keep up with it.

This is easier than you think. It is pretty simple to keep up with your money because you know your buy-in when you start. For the casino poker table, you write down the date and how much money you start with. If you are reaching in your pocket for more money or go to the ATM, you need to record that as well. The best way is to keep a log.

It is really simple but does require some discipline. I have tried to make this simpler by creating a Poker Log spreadsheet that can be downloaded off of my website at **www.pokerdeductions.com**, or you are welcome to copy the one in this chapter.

Whether on-line or physically at a poker table, write down the date, and the time you start playing. If you are on the wait list, I would start counting your time while you are waiting (as long as the wait time is reasonable). When you start to play, be sure to write down exactly how much you start with. It is also extremely important to write down any money added during this session. Most casinos will not let you take money off the table (except to tip the drink server). Therefore, you truly can measure your win/loss amount by counting your money when leaving the table.

The fact is that if you keep a log, even by hand, you are able to produce this as your substantiation to the IRS in the event of an audit.

It is important to keep the log "as you go". There have been many cases where the IRS has been able to prove that a log was done many years after the tax return was prepared. Their opinion on this is that it is impossible to accurately reconstruct events that happened many years later. They also know that people do this only after they received notice of an audit.

My suggestion is to use the log sample in this book each time you gamble. Write down your activity and then transfer the information to your spreadsheet and have formulas in so that you can have the computer total your win/loss amounts and your time at the table. Keeping the time is important to show the amount of hours you work in your business. Be sure to keep your handwritten pages for future proof if needed. It is important to list the casino or internet site where you play. This provides further substantiation of where you are, especially to back up any expenses based on your location.

One other suggestion is to write down the type of table, i.e. 20/40 limit, tournament, etc. and the casino in which you are playing.

POKER LOG BOOK

MONTH OF _____, 200__

DATE	TIME IN	TIME OUT	TIME PLAYED	CASH IN	CASH OUT	TOTAL WIN (LOSS)	TYPE TABLE	LOCATION

Poker Log Page

Not only do you need to keep records of your play, you also need to keep other expense records. Another crucial area is your Auto Expenses (See Chapter 6). Here is an example of a way to keep track of this:

Mileage Log

Date	Odometer Start	Odometer End	Trip Mileage	Business Purpose

Total Miles [   ]

Business Miles [   ]

Auto Mileage Spreadsheet

This spreadsheet can also be downloaded off my website www.pokerdeductions.com for your use. It's one of the easiest ways to keep up with mileage on your vehicle that you used for your business.

Keeping up with your other business expenses is easier if you use a credit card. It is better to have a credit card that you use just for your business expenses. That way it is easier to keep up with expenses during the year. It makes it hard to have to try to remember whether you charged something, paid cash or wrote a check. Many of the credit card companies give you a summary at year end which makes it so much easier to get prepared for tax time.

If you use a checkbook to pay for expenses, you need to keep a register. You also need to keep your canceled checks as further proof of payment as well as any accompanying receipts to show the expense detail. Be sure to identify in your checkbook (or in your computer program if you use one) where your deposit came from, i.e. income, loan, gift, etc.

Always keep your business transactions separate from your personal transactions. If you need money, such as out of your checking account, be sure to write the check to yourself. This way you know exactly where the money went. If you have to write a check to cash to pay for a business expense, include the receipt for the cash payment in your records. If you cannot get a receipt for a cash payment, you should make an adequate explanation in your records at the time of payment.

Another way to keep up with your records is to use one of the off-the-shelf accounting programs that you can buy at your local office supply store. Most are relatively easy to use and require very little bookkeeping knowledge. The program will be able to help you combine expenses from several areas automatically, such as your checkbook and your credit card statements once you have entered them into the system.

How long should you keep these records? This is a common question that people ask me. This is not necessarily an easy one to answer. It falls into the "it depends" category. The standard answer is to keep your records as long as they may be needed for the administration of any provision of the Internal Revenue Code. Huh?

You need to keep records to support items on your return for the period of time in which you can amend your return, claim a credit or a refund, or the IRS can assess additional tax. I basically advise seven to ten years to be on the safe side.

This may be a challenge. If you find that you continue for several years to not turn a profit, formulate a specific plan on how you intend to change your pattern. Changing a bad run on cards can be difficult. Perhaps show that you are investing time in research to change your playing style. Take classes on how to interpret body language. Consult with another pro. These are a few examples of what the IRS would be looking for.

I'M TIRED – LET'S RETIRE!

♠ ♥ ♣ ♦

Finally back in Vegas. Even as the plane starts its approach into the airport, I get such a rush I feel like I am going to explode. I felt as if one minute lost without being on a table would be the worst thing in the world. Once I drop my luggage in the room, I am down at the poker room in no time. This trip is different though. I went over and above for a client. My reward? He added $5000 to my bill as a "thank you." Found money, I say. So this time I walk to the podium in the middle because I want to sit up at the high limit tables. Scared to death, I walk up and take a seat. As I look around, I see a woman that looks familiar. Then it hits me – it is her, all right, straight off the TV poker pro games. I try not to look as petrified as I am and after a couple of rounds, I feel at ease. It's the same as my $20/$40 games, just a hell of a lot more money at stake.

When she found out what I did for a living, she said "I hate to ask but I was wondering if you had any advice on how to set up retirement?" "Of course," I replied. "Tell me how you have your business structured." She told me she was structured as a Schedule C for her poker playing. "Retirement is fairly simple and with your income, you can start putting away a lot of money fairly quickly. I will map it all out for you tonight and e-mail a summary to you." "Great", she said, "but you might be mad at me after this hand."

The flop was showing 9 9 Jack, the turn showed a 7. She and I were heads up and the pot had about $4,000 in it. I had Jack 9 in the hole. The river came a King. I smiled and turned over J 9 – nines full of jacks. She smiled bigger and showed King King – kings full of nines. "Well," I said as I stood up. "I guess I better summarize that for you and stick to what I know best."

Poker and Retirement. Yes, you can do it. You don't have to be a big company any longer to set up a retirement plan. When you are self-employed, it's really simple to set up an IRA or a SEP plan and start contributing.

TRADITIONAL IRA

How do you do this? The easy way that anyone can do is a Traditional IRA. You just have to have earned income (which is income that you earn from sources such as your poker business (it has to show a profit) or other earnings such as a W2. It does not include investments such as interest and dividends. So, as long as you earned at least $3,000, you can take up to $3,000 off of your tax return for an IRA deduction.

SEP PLAN

What if you want to do more? Another way is by setting up a plan called a SEP (Self Employed Pension). This is customarily set up with a brokerage firm. They keep up with the money in a pre-tax account. What is that? Well, it is an account that, when you put money into it, you are basically telling the brokerage company that you did not pay tax on this money. The way that you do not pay tax on it is getting a "direct" deduction from your income on your tax return. This is taken on the front page of the Form 1040 as an adjustment to income. Therefore, it is "pre-tax" money.

What this also means is that the money, once you put it into this account, is taxed WITH PENALTIES if you take it out before you are 59 ½ years old. This is to discourage you from taking it out!

I am assuming in the SEP discussion that you are a poker player filing the Schedule C with no employees. In order to deduct for retirement, you have to show a profit. The SEP is calculated based on the amount of profit that your business is showing on the tax return.

First of all, let's look at the advantages of doing a SEP:

- ✓ Easy to set up
- ✓ Contributions are tax deductible
- ✓ No annual reporting requirements to the IRS
- ✓ Once you put money into the plan, you decide what investments that it goes to
- ✓ You are immediately vested
- ✓ You don't have to contribute each year if you don't want to
- ✓ Maximum contributions are generally greater than doing a Traditional IRA
- ✓ Can still make deductible contributions after age 70 ½
- ✓ Can establish the plan up to the due date of your tax return, plus extensions
- ✓ You can rollover the money into another pre-tax plan with a different brokerage firm

Sounds pretty good but where there are advantages, there are disadvantages:

- ✗ If you contribute when you are young, you have a longer time to wait to withdraw the money
- ✗ Emergencies may tempt you to withdraw money before age 59 ½
- ✗ Early withdraws have a 10% penalty plus you have to pay your current Federal tax rate (and State if applicable) on the funds taken
- ✗ You cannot borrow against the money you have contributed to the plan

So, you decide that this SEP plan is for you. You want to set up a plan but what is the maximum amount that you can put into it? The amount is determined by looking at your Schedule C net income. This is the number on the front of your tax return on the line that says "Business income or loss. Attach Schedule C or C-EZ". Take this number and subtract from it ½ of your Self-employment tax deduction. This is the number that calculates on the front of your tax return under the adjustment section that says "One-half of self-employment tax. Attach Schedule SE". Once you have subtracted this, multiply it by 20%. As long as this number is less than $42,000 (the maximum amount for 2005-this changes each year), then that is the maximum you can contribute and then take as a deduction.

Let's do a very basic tax return example.

EXAMPLE 4:

Bob Mann has the following on his tax return:

Gambling Income	$100,000

Business Expenses:

Amounts paid in wagering	$35,000
Estimated taxes paid 4/15/05	$17,000

Bob wants to contribute as much as possible to his retirement plan. Based on the below, he can contribute up to $12,082. This was calculated by taking his net profit of $65,000, subtracting ½ of self-employment tax and then multiplying by 20%.

The following is how this example would be reported on your tax return.

Example 4:

Form **1040**	U.S. Individual Income Tax Return			(99)	IRS Use Only - Do not write or staple in this space.

Label
(See instructions on page 16.)
Use the IRS label.
Otherwise, please print or type.

L A B E L H E R E

		For the year Jan. 1-Dec. 31, , or other tax year beginning , ending , 20	OMB No. 1545-0074
Your first name and initial	Last name		Your social security number
BOB	MANN		777 00 2222
If a joint return, spouse's first name and initial	Last name		Spouse's social security number
Home address (number and street). If you have a P.O. box, see page 16.		Apt. no.	▲ **Important!** ▲
9999 EASY STREET			You **must** enter
City, town or post office, state, and ZIP code. If you have a foreign address, see page 16.			your SSN(s) above.
BYTEME, GA 10000			

Presidential Election Campaign
(See page 16.) ▶ Note. Checking "Yes" will not change your tax or reduce your refund.

Do you, or your spouse if filing a joint return, want $3 to go to this fund? ▶ **You** [ ] Yes [X] No **Spouse** [ ] Yes [ ] No

Filing Status
Check only one box.

1 [X] Single
2 [ ] Married filing jointly (even if only one had income)
3 [ ] Married filing separately. Enter spouse's SSN above and full name here. ▶
4 [ ] Head of household (with qualifying person). (See page 17.) If the qualifying person is a child but not your dependent, enter this child's name here. ▶
5 [ ] Qualifying widow(er) with dependent child (see page 17)

Exemptions

6a [X] Yourself. If someone can claim you as a dependent, **do not** check box 6a ....
b [ ] Spouse

c Dependents:		(2) Dependent's social security number	(3) Dependent's relationship to you	(4) ✓ If qualifying child for child tax credit (see page 18)
(1) First name	Last name			

Boxes checked on 6a and 6b **1**

No. of children on 6c who:
• lived with you
• did not live with you due to divorce or separation (see page 18)

If more than four dependents, see page 18.

Dependents on 6c not entered above

d Total number of exemptions claimed ....

Add numbers on lines above ▶ **1**

Income

Attach Form(s) W-2 here. Also attach Forms W-2G and 1099-R if tax was withheld.

If you did not get a W-2, see page 19.

Enclose, but do not attach, any payment. Also, please use Form 1040-V.

7	Wages, salaries, tips, etc. Attach Form(s) W-2		7	
8a	Taxable interest. Attach Schedule B if required		8a	
b	Tax-exempt interest. **Do not** include on line 8a	8b		
9a	Ordinary dividends. Attach Schedule B if required		9a	
b	Qualified dividends (see page 20)	9b		
10	Taxable refunds, credits, or offsets of state and local income taxes		10	
11	Alimony received		11	
12	Business income or (loss). Attach Schedule C or C-EZ		12	65,000.
13	Capital gain or (loss). Attach Schedule D if required. If not required, check here ▶ [ ]		13	
14	Other gains or (losses). Attach Form 4797		14	
15a	IRA distributions	15a	b Taxable amount (see page 22)	15b	
16a	Pensions and annuities	16a	b Taxable amount (see page 22)	16b	
17	Rental real estate, royalties, partnerships, S corporations, trusts, etc. Attach Schedule E		17	
18	Farm income or (loss). Attach Schedule F		18	
19	Unemployment compensation		19	
20a	Social security benefits	20a	b Taxable amount (see page 24)	20b	
21	Other income. List type and amount (see page 24)		21	
22	Add the amounts in the far right column for lines 7 through 21. This is your **total income** ▶		22	65,000.

Adjusted Gross Income

23	Educator expenses (see page 26)	23		
24	Certain business expenses of reservists, performing artists, and fee-basis government officials. Attach Form 2106 or 2106-EZ	24		
25	IRA deduction (see page 26)	25		
26	Student loan interest deduction (see page 28)	26		
27	Tuition and fees deduction (see page 29)	27		
28	Health savings account deduction. Attach Form 8889	28		
29	Moving expenses. Attach Form 3903	29		
30	One-half of self-employment tax. Attach Schedule SE	30	4,592.	
31	Self-employed health insurance deduction (see page 30)	31		
32	Self-employed SEP, SIMPLE, and qualified plans	32	12,082.	
33	Penalty on early withdrawal of savings	33		
34a	Alimony paid b Recipient's SSN ▶	34a		
35	Add lines 23 through 34a		35	16,674.
36	Subtract line 35 from line 22. This is your **adjusted gross income** ▶		36	48,326.

410001
11-03-04

LHA **For Disclosure, Privacy Act, and Paperwork Reduction Act Notice, see page 75.**

Form 1040

Example 4:

	Form 1040	BOB MANN		777-00-2222		Page 2
Tax and	37	Amount from line 36 (adjusted gross income)			37	48,326.
Credits	38a	Check { You were born before January 2, 1940, ☐ Blind. **Total boxes**				
Standard		if: { Spouse was born before January 2, 1940, ☐ Blind. } **checked** ▶ 38a ☐				
Deduction for -	b	If your spouse itemizes on a separate return or you were a dual-status alien, see page 31 and check here ▶ 38b ☐				
● People who checked any box on line 38a or 38b **or** who can be claimed as a dependent.	39	**Itemized deductions** (from Schedule A) or your **standard deduction** (see left margin)			39	5,000.
	40	Subtract line 39 from line 37			40	43,326.
	41	If line 37 is $107,025 or less, multiply $3,100 by the total number of exemptions claimed on line 6d. If line 37 is over $107,025, see the worksheet on page 33			41	3,200.
● All others:	42	**Taxable income.** Subtract line 41 from line 40. If line 41 is more than line 40, enter -0-			42	40,126.
Single or Married filing separately, $4,850	43	**Tax.** Check if any tax is from: **a** ☐ Form(s) 8814 **b** ☐ Form 4972			43	6,769.
	44	**Alternative minimum tax.** Attach Form 6251			44	
Married filing jointly or Qualifying widow(er), $9,700	45	Add lines 43 and 44		▶	45	6,769.
	46	Foreign tax credit. Attach Form 1116 if required		46		
	47	Credit for child and dependent care expenses. Attach Form 2441		47		
Head of household, $7,150	48	Credit for the elderly or the disabled. Attach Schedule R		48		
	49	Education credits. Attach Form 8863		49		
	50	Retirement savings contributions credit. Attach Form 8880		50		
	51	Child tax credit (see page 37)		51		
	52	Adoption credit. Attach Form 8839		52		
	53	Credits from: **a** ☐ Form 8396 **b** ☐ Form 8859		53		
	54	Other credits. Check applicable box(es): **a** ☐ Form 3800				
		b ☐ Form 8801 **c** ☐ Specify		54		
	55	Add lines 46 through 54. These are your **total credits**			55	
	56	Subtract line 55 from line 45. If line 55 is more than line 45, enter -0-		▶	56	6,769.
Other Taxes	57	Self-employment tax. Attach Schedule SE			57	9,184.
	58	Social security and Medicare tax on tip income not reported to employer. Attach Form 4137			58	
	59	Additional tax on IRAs, other qualified retirement plans, etc. Attach Form 5329 if required			59	
	60	Advance earned income credit payments from Form(s) W-2			60	
	61	Household employment taxes. Attach Schedule H			61	
	62	Add lines 56 through 61. This is your **total tax**		▶	62	15,953.
Payments	63	Federal income tax withheld from Forms W-2 and 1099		63		
	64	2004 estimated tax payments and amount applied from 2003 return		64	17,000.	
If you have a qualifying child, attach Schedule EIC.	65a	**Earned income credit (EIC)**		65a		
	b	Nontaxable combat pay election ▶	65b			
	66	Excess social security and tier 1 RRTA tax withheld (see page 54)		66		
	67	Additional child tax credit. Attach Form 8812		67		
	68	Amount paid with request for extension to file (see page 54)		68		
	69	Other payments from: **a** ☐ Form 2439 **b** ☐ Form 4136 **c** ☐ Form 8885		69		
	70	Add lines 63, 64, 65a, and 66 through 69. These are your **total payments**		▶	70	17,000.
Refund	71	If line 70 is more than line 62, subtract line 62 from line 70. This is the amount you **overpaid**			71	1,047.
Direct deposit? See page 54 and fill in 72b, 72c, and 72d.	72a	Amount of line 71 you want **refunded to you**		▶	72a	1,047.
	b	Routing number ▶ **c** Type: ☐ Checking ☐ Savings ▶ **d** Account number ▶				
	73	Amount of line 71 you want **applied to your 2005 estimated tax** ▶	73			
Amount	74	**Amount you owe.** Subtract line 70 from line 62. For details on how to pay, see page 55		▶	74	
You Owe	75	Estimated tax penalty (see page 55)		75		
Third Party		Do you want to allow another person to discuss this return with the IRS (see page 56)? ☐ **Yes.** Complete the following. ☐ **No**				
Designee		Designee's name ▶	Phone no. ▶		Personal identification number (PIN) ▶	

Sign Here
Joint return? See page 17. Keep a copy for your records.

Under penalties of perjury, I declare that I have examined this return and accompanying schedules and statements, and to the best of my knowledge and belief, they are true, correct, and complete. Declaration of preparer (other than taxpayer) is based on all information of which preparer has any knowledge.

Your signature	Date	Your occupation	Daytime phone number
▶			
Spouse's signature. If a joint return, **both** must sign.	Date	Spouse's occupation	

Paid Preparer's Use Only

Preparer's signature ▶		Date	Check if self-employed ☐	Preparer's SSN or PTIN
Firm's name (or yours if self-employed), address, and ZIP code			EIN	
			Phone no.	

410002
11-03-04

How To Turn Your Poker Playing Into A Business

Example 4:

SCHEDULE C (Form 1040)	**Profit or Loss From Business**	OMB No. 1545-0074
Department of the Treasury Internal Revenue Service	(Sole Proprietorship) ▶ Partnerships, joint ventures, etc., must file Form 1065 or 1065-B. ▶ Attach to Form 1040 or 1041. ▶See Instructions for Schedule C (Form 1040).	Attachment Sequence No. 09

Name of proprietor: **BOB MANN**

Social security number (SSN): **777-00-2222**

A Principal business or profession, including product or service (see page C-2): **GAMBLING/WAGERING**

B Enter code from pages C-7, 8, & 9 ▶ **999999**

C Business name. If no separate business name, leave blank.

D Employer ID number (EIN), if any

E Business address (including suite or room no.) ▶

City, town or post office, state, and ZIP code

F Accounting method: (1) [X] Cash (2) [ ] Accrual (3) [ ] Other (specify) ▶

G Did you "materially participate" in the operation of this business during 2004? If "No," see page C-3 for limit on losses ... [X] Yes [ ] No

H If you started or acquired this business during 2004, check here ▶ [ ]

Part I Income

1	Gross receipts or sales. **Caution.** If this income was reported to you on Form W-2 and the "Statutory employee" box on that form was checked, see page C-3 and check here ▶ [ ]	1	100,000.
2	Returns and allowances	2	
3	Subtract line 2 from line 1	3	100,000.
4	Cost of goods sold (from line 42 on page 2)	4	35,000.
5	**Gross profit.** Subtract line 4 from line 3	5	65,000.
6	Other income, including Federal and state gasoline or fuel tax credit or refund (see page C-3)	6	
7	**Gross income.** Add lines 5 and 6 ▶	7	65,000.

Part II Expenses. Enter expenses for business use of your home only on line 30.

8	Advertising	8		19	Pension and profit-sharing plans	19
9	Car and truck expenses (see page C-3)	9		20	Rent or lease (see page C-5):	
10	Commissions and fees	10		a	Vehicles, machinery, and equipment	20a
11	Contract labor (see page C-4)	11		b	Other business property	20b
12	Depletion	12		21	Repairs and maintenance	21
13	Depreciation and section 179 expense deduction (not included in Part III) (see page C-4)	13		22	Supplies (not included in Part III)	22
				23	Taxes and licenses	23
14	Employee benefit programs (other than on line 19)	14		24	Travel, meals, and entertainment:	
15	Insurance (other than health)	15		a	Travel	24a
16	Interest:			b	Meals and entertainment	
a	Mortgage (paid to banks, etc.)	16a		c	Enter nondeductible amount included on line 24b (see page C-5)	
b	Other	16b		d	Subtract line 24c from line 24b	24d
17	Legal and professional services	17		25	Utilities	25
18	Office expense	18		26	Wages (less employment credits)	26
				27	Other expenses (from line 48 on page 2)	27

28	**Total expenses** before expenses for business use of home. Add lines 8 through 27 in columns ▶	28	0.
29	Tentative profit (loss). Subtract line 28 from line 7	29	65,000.
30	Expenses for business use of your home. Attach Form 8829	30	
31	**Net profit or (loss).** Subtract line 30 from line 29.		
	• If a profit, enter on **Form 1040, line 12,** and **also** on **Schedule SE, line 2** (statutory employees, see page C-6). Estates and trusts, enter on Form 1041, line 3.	31	65,000.
	• If a loss, you **must** go to line 32.		
32	If you have a loss, check the box that describes your investment in this activity (see page C-6).		
	• If you checked 32a, enter the loss on **Form 1040, line 12,** and **also** on **Schedule SE, line 2** (statutory employees, see page C-6). Estates and trusts, enter on Form 1041, line 3.	32a	[ ] All investment is at risk.
	• If you checked 32b, you **must** attach Form 6198.	32b	[ ] Some investment is not at risk.

LHA For Paperwork Reduction Act Notice, see Form 1040 instructions.

Schedule C (Form 1040)

420001 11-03-04

Example 4:

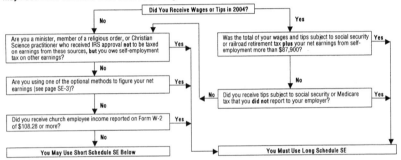

SCHEDULE SE
(Form 1040)

Department of the Treasury
Internal Revenue Service

Self-Employment Tax

▶ Attach to Form 1040. ▶ See Instructions for Schedule SE (Form 1040).

OMB No. 1545-0074

Attachment
Sequence No. **17**

Name of person with **self-employment** income (as shown on Form 1040)

BOB MANN

Social security number of
person with **self-employment**
income .... ▶ 777 ¦ 00 ¦ 2222

Who Must File Schedule SE

You must file Schedule SE if:

● You had net earnings from self-employment from **other than** church employee income (line 4 of Short Schedule SE or line 4c of Long Schedule SE) of $400 or more **or**

● You had church employee income of $108.28 or more. Income from services you performed as a minister or a member of a religious order **is not** church employee income (see page SE-1).

Note. Even if you had a loss or a small amount of income from self-employment, it may be to your benefit to file Schedule SE and use either "optional method" in Part II of Long Schedule SE (see page SE-3).

Exception. If your only self-employment income was from earnings as a minister, member of a religious order, or Christian Science practitioner **and** you filed Form 4361 and received IRS approval not to be taxed on those earnings, **do not** file Schedule SE. Instead, write "Exempt-Form 4361" on Form 1040, line 57.

May I Use Short Schedule SE or Must I Use Long Schedule SE?

Did You Receive Wages or Tips in 2004?

No ← → Yes

Are you a minister, member of a religious order, or Christian Science practitioner who received IRS approval **not** to be taxed on earnings from these sources, **but** you owe self-employment tax on other earnings? → Yes ▶

Was the total of your wages and tips subject to social security or railroad retirement tax **plus** your net earnings from self-employment more than $87,900? → Yes ▶

No ↓

Are you using one of the optional methods to figure your net earnings (see page SE-3)? → Yes ▶

No ↓

No → Did you receive tips subject to social security or Medicare tax that you **did not** report to your employer? → Yes ▶

No ↓

Did you receive church employee income reported on Form W-2 of $108.28 or more? → Yes ▶

No ↓

You May Use Short Schedule SE Below

→ **You Must Use Long Schedule SE**

Section A-Short Schedule SE. Caution. Read above to see if you can use Short Schedule SE.

1 Net farm profit or (loss) from Schedule F, line 36, and farm partnerships, Schedule K-1 (Form 1065), box 14, code A	**1**	
2 Net profit or (loss) from Schedule C, line 31; Schedule C-EZ, line 3; Schedule K-1 (Form 1065), box 14, code A (other than farming); and Schedule K-1 (Form 1065-B), box 9. Ministers and members of religious orders. see page SE-1 for amounts to report on this line. See page SE-2 for other income to report	**2**	65,000.
3 Combine lines 1 and 2	**3**	65,000.
4 **Net earnings from self-employment.** Multiply line 3 by 92.35% (.9235). If less than $400, **do not** file this schedule; you do not owe self-employment tax ..... ▶	**4**	60,028.
5 **Self-employment tax.** If the amount on line 4 is: ● $87,900 or less, multiply line 4 by 15.3% (.153). Enter the result here and on **Form 1040, line 57.** ● More than $87,900, multiply line 4 by 2.9% (.029). Then, add $10,899.60 to the result. Enter the total here and on **Form 1040, line 57.**	**5**	9,184.
6 Deduction for one-half of self-employment tax. Multiply line 5 by 50% (.5). Enter the result here and on **Form 1040, line 30** ..... **6** | 4,592.		

LHA For Paperwork Reduction Act Notice, see Form 1040 instructions.

Schedule SE (Form 1040)

424501
10-27-04

How To Turn Your Poker Playing Into A Business

Example 4:

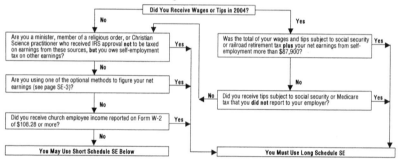

SCHEDULE SE
(Form 1040)

Department of the Treasury
Internal Revenue Service

Self-Employment Tax

▶ Attach to Form 1040. ▶ See Instructions for Schedule SE (Form 1040).

OMB No. 1545-0074

Attachment
Sequence No. **17**

Name of person with **self-employment** income (as shown on Form 1040)

BOB MANN

Social security number of person with **self-employment** income ▶ 777 00 2222

Who Must File Schedule SE

You must file Schedule SE if:

- You had net earnings from self-employment from **other than** church employee income (line 4 of Short Schedule SE or line 4c of Long Schedule SE) of $400 or more **or**
- You had church employee income of $108.28 or more. Income from services you performed as a minister or a member of a religious order **is not** church employee income (see page SE-1).

Note. Even if you had a loss or a small amount of income from self-employment, it may be to your benefit to file Schedule SE and use either "optional method" in Part II of Long Schedule SE (see page SE-3).

Exception. If your only self-employment income was from earnings as a minister, member of a religious order, or Christian Science practitioner **and** you filed Form 4361 and received IRS approval not to be taxed on those earnings, **do not** file Schedule SE. Instead, write "Exempt-Form 4361" on Form 1040, line 57.

May I Use Short Schedule SE or Must I Use Long Schedule SE?

Did You Receive Wages or Tips in 2004?

No → Are you a minister, member of a religious order, or Christian Science practitioner who received IRS approval **not** to be taxed on earnings from these sources, **but** you owe self-employment tax on other earnings?

Yes → Was the total of your wages and tips subject to social security or railroad retirement tax **plus** your net earnings from self-employment more than $87,900?

No ↓ Are you using one of the optional methods to figure your net earnings (see page SE-3)?

Yes → No ← Did you receive tips subject to social security or Medicare tax that you **did not** report to your employer?

No ↓ Did you receive church employee income reported on Form W-2 of $108.28 or more?

No ↓

You May Use Short Schedule SE Below

You Must Use Long Schedule SE

Section A-Short Schedule SE. Caution. Read above to see if you can use Short Schedule SE.

1 Net farm profit or (loss) from Schedule F, line 36, and farm partnerships, Schedule K-1 (Form 1065), box 14, code A	1	
2 Net profit or (loss) from Schedule C, line 31; Schedule C-EZ, line 3; Schedule K-1 (Form 1065), box 14, code A (other than farming); and Schedule K-1 (Form 1065-B), box 9. Ministers and members of religious orders. see page SE-1 for amounts to report on this line. See page SE-2 for other income to report	2	65,000.
3 Combine lines 1 and 2	3	65,000.
4 **Net earnings from self-employment.** Multiply line 3 by 92.35% (.9235). If less than $400, **do not** file this schedule; you do not owe self-employment tax ▶	4	60,028.
5 **Self-employment tax.** If the amount on line 4 is:		
• $87,900 or less, multiply line 4 by 15.3% (.153). Enter the result here and on **Form 1040, line 57.**	5	9,184.
• More than $87,900, multiply line 4 by 2.9% (.029). Then, add $10,899.60 to the result. Enter the total here and on **Form 1040, line 57.**		
6 **Deduction for one-half of self-employment tax.** Multiply line 5 by 50% (.5). Enter the result here and on **Form 1040, line 30**	6	4,592.

LHA   For Paperwork Reduction Act Notice, see Form 1040 instructions.

Schedule SE (Form 1040)

424501
10-27-04

84

TAKING YOUR POKER
TO ANOTHER LEVEL

♠ ♥ ♣ ♦

I went over to Rob's for a local poker tournament. The first Wednesday of the month there is a $100 buy-in and about 35 people show up. There are all kinds of players. You have Sid who won't shut up and knows all the rules to David who is just a nice guy looking for something to do.

While Rob gets the chips in order and logs us all into the tournament software program, I start socializing with the guys. There are two other women that play and we know several of the new guys are looking at us as if to say "why are you here?" Oh well – that's the way some are.

Mark was there. He played (and placed) in the big tournament last year and used part of his winnings to write a book on poker strategy. I happened to be seated at Mark's table and was able to ask about how his book was going.

"Great," he said, "I'm actually starting to get about 3,500 orders a month." "Did you form a corporation for this" I asked. "No, I just wasn't sure what I should do and have been including it in my Schedule C for my professional poker playing."

"That is definitely not a good idea," I told him. "Those are two different businesses with different sets of rules, and, your loss rules are different" I replied. "Tell me more," Mark said.

So, you are a pro on TV and are more popular than you ever imagined. Why not promote the world of poker and help your fellow man by writing a book, having an informative website or selling other types of poker merchandise?

Even if you aren't the best, or if people have never really heard of you, going a step further by doing something other than "playing cards" may be a great money maker. (Sound familiar?)

> **NOTE: If you branch out into a business besides poker or gambling/wagering, I highly recommend that you have a different company for this purpose. In doing a business besides wagering, you are now under a different, and somewhat better, set of rules. Now you are actually allowed to deduct losses that are not allowed under the gambling rules.**

If you want to keep this simple, you can always do this on a separate Schedule C on your tax return. Yes, you can have two (or more) Schedule C's and you should when you have different types of businesses. The income and expenses work similar to the way I have described earlier in the book with a few exceptions.

First, the biggest difference is that you are allowed to have losses. Now remember that with losses, you cannot do a SEP retirement plan as described in Chapter 9. You are also limited in your health insurance adjustment that is on the front page of your tax return.

You need to be mindful of losses for too many years. Remember that the IRS can basically put you out of business if you go more than 2-3 years without profits. An exception may be if you formulate a plan to turn your business around.

So you are going to do a separate business from your gambling but have heard that you should protect yourself with a corporation. How true is this and what are your options?

There are many ways to file your business. When you want to go a separate route from filing it with your personal tax return, you are open to more stricter reporting requirements to the IRS and you truly have to operate as a separate entity.

Summarized below are the basics describing the different types of entities that you can form for your business. You should also consult with your accountant and/or attorney for further assistance.

CORPORATION (ALSO CALLED C-CORP)

This is an entity that has its own legal status that is separate from its owners. A corporation may be difficult and expensive to organize. Corporations have to hold board meetings and keep minutes as well as comply with Federal and State regulations. They have corporate charters that restrict the type of business activity that they can perform.

A Corporation pays tax on its profits. When the owners (shareholders) take profits from the company, they are taxed a dividends, which is double taxation. The corporation has to file a tax return with the IRS which has more complex reporting than a Schedule C. There are also more accounting fees associated with filing a corporate tax return.

SMALL BUSINESS CORPORATION
(REFERRED TO AS S-CORPORATION)

This form of business is set up like a regular C-Corporation. It then elects to be treated as an S-Corporation by filing Form 2553 (Election by a Small Business Corporation). Only domestic corporations with one class of stock are eligible to be taxed as an S-Corporation and it is limited to having 100 shareholders.

An S-Corporation it taxed similar to a partnership to where the profit or loss flows through to the shareholder tax return. The profits that flow to the shareholder are not subject to Self-Employment tax but are subject to Federal taxation (state tax may also apply). Shareholders pay tax on all of the earnings of the S-Corporation whether they distribute the profits or not. A shareholder that works for the S-Corporation receives a reasonable salary for work performed.

PARTNERSHIP

A partnership is an organization that has two or more owners. Partnership profits or losses flow to the shareholder and are subject to Self-Employment tax as well as Federal tax (state tax may also apply).

A partnership is relatively easy to organize. It is not required but is recommended that a written agreement exist between the partners to address the terms of the relationship. In a partnership, general partners are liable for the actions of the other partners.

LIMITED LIABILITY COMPANY (LLC)

This is an entity formed under state law that combines the pass-through tax of a partnership with the limited liability of a corporation. The income and expenses flow through to the "members" and the profit may be subject to self-employment tax. The members can be any person or entity including an individual, corporation, partnership or other LLC or trust.

The LLC is taxed as a partnership but remember, if there is only one "member", the LLC is filed on a Schedule C and NOT on a Partnership Tax Return.

You can elect for the LLC to be taxed as a corporation by filing a Form 8832 (Entity Classification Election) and you can even go so far as to have it taxed as an S-Corporation with Form 2553 (Election by a Small Business Corporation).

The degree of personal liability protection for the members of an LLC differ from state to state.

DOING YOUR TAX RETURN

♠ ♥ ♣ ♦

Ronnie came into my office with a big box. "What is this?" I asked. "This is everything I did in my poker business last year. I just piled it all in a box for you to sort it out."

"You know," I replied, "It will cost more for me to go through this for you as opposed to you totaling things for me. I also charge extra for the massive cat hair that I see floating out of the box. This is gross!" "Hey," he laughed, "I used this box all year to pile receipts in. I can't help it if my cat likes to sleep on my tax work!"

I sat down on April 12th, with receipts and cat hair all over my desk, wishing I were at a poker table instead.

Now that I have told you what can or cannot be deducted on a tax return, let's prepare some examples that you may be able to relate to. These returns are much different from the returns we did in Chapter 3 when you were a hobby. Believe it or not, these returns were very simple. Making your poker playing a business is a bit of a challenge when it comes to a tax return, but I will try to keep it as basic as possible.

People that are gambling for a living, i.e. as a business, need to file a Schedule C (Profit or Loss from Business) with their personal tax return (Form 1040). The better records you keep during the year, the happier you (or your accountant) will be later. Here are some examples:

EXAMPLE 5 - BUSINESS TAX RETURN

Harry Jones is a professional poker player that meets the facts and circumstances test, blah, blah, blah, to treat his poker playing as a business. He is single with no dependents and cannot itemize. Here is what he has:

Gambling Income	$70,000
Business Expenses:	
Amounts Paid in Wagering	$35,000
Business Cards	$25
Office Supplies	$275
Accounting Fees	$350
Business License	$75
Bank Charges	$60
Poker Books	$250
Internet Fees	$600
Cell Phone	$1,500
Meals/Entertainment	$4,000

Travel $8,000

Mileage-business   9,600

(using 2004 rate of 37 ¹/₂ cents per mile)

Estimated taxes paid during the year on Form 1040-ES:

Paid 4/15 $2,000

Paid 6/15 $2,000

Paid 9/15 $2,000

Paid 1/15 of the following year $2,000

Example 5:

Form **1040**	U.S. Individual Income Tax Return	(99)	IRS Use Only - Do not write or staple in this space.

For the year Jan. 1-Dec. 31, , or other tax year beginning , ending , 20   OMB No. 1545-0074

Label (See instructions on page 16.)

Your first name and initial: **HARRY**   Last name: **JONES**   Your social security number: **777 88 9999**

If a joint return, spouse's first name and initial   Last name   Spouse's social security number

Home address (number and street). If you have a P.O. box, see page 16.: **4444 QUAD COURT**   Apt. no.

City, town or post office, state, and ZIP code. If you have a foreign address, see page 16.: **RAINBOW, GA 99888**

▲ **Important!** ▲ You **must** enter your SSN(s) above.

Presidential Election Campaign (See page 16.) Note. Checking "Yes" will not change your tax or reduce your refund. Do you, or your spouse if filing a joint return, want $3 to go to this fund?   You: Yes ☐ No [X]   Spouse: Yes ☐ No ☐

Filing Status — Check only one box.
1 [X] Single
2 ☐ Married filing jointly (even if only one had income)
3 ☐ Married filing separately. Enter spouse's SSN above and full name here. ▶
4 ☐ Head of household (with qualifying person). (See page 17.) If the qualifying person is a child but not your dependent, enter this child's name here. ▶
5 ☐ Qualifying widow(er) with dependent child (see page 17)

Exemptions
6a [X] Yourself. If someone can claim you as a dependent, **do not** check box 6a
b ☐ Spouse

Boxes checked on 6a and 6b: **1**

c Dependents:
(1) First name / Last name | (2) Dependent's social security number | (3) Dependent's relationship to you | (4) ✓ if qualifying child for child tax credit (see page 18)

No. of children on 6c who: ● lived with you ● did not live with you due to divorce or separation (see page 18)

Dependents on 6c not entered above

If more than four dependents, see page 18.

d Total number of exemptions claimed   Add numbers on lines above ▶ **1**

Income

Attach Form(s) W-2 here. Also attach Forms W-2G and 1099-R if tax was withheld.

7 Wages, salaries, tips, etc. Attach Form(s) W-2 — 7
8a Taxable interest. Attach Schedule B if required — 8a
b Tax-exempt interest. Do not include on line 8a — 8b
9a Ordinary dividends. Attach Schedule B if required — 9a
b Qualified dividends (see page 20) — 9b
10 Taxable refunds, credits, or offsets of state and local income taxes — 10
11 Alimony received — 11
12 Business income or (loss). Attach Schedule C or C-EZ — 12 **33,265.**
13 Capital gain or (loss). Attach Schedule D if required. If not required, check here ▶ ☐ — 13
14 Other gains or (losses). Attach Form 4797 — 14
15a IRA distributions — 15a b Taxable amount (see page 22) — 15b
16a Pensions and annuities — 16a b Taxable amount (see page 22) — 16b
17 Rental real estate, royalties, partnerships, S corporations, trusts, etc. Attach Schedule E — 17
18 Farm income or (loss). Attach Schedule F — 18
19 Unemployment compensation — 19
20a Social security benefits — 20a b Taxable amount (see page 24) — 20b
21 Other income. List type and amount (see page 24) — 21
22 Add the amounts in the far right column for lines 7 through 21. This is your **total income** ▶ — 22 **33,265.**

If you did not get a W-2, see page 19. Enclose, but do not attach, any payment. Also, please use Form 1040-V.

Adjusted Gross Income
23 Educator expenses (see page 26) — 23
24 Certain business expenses of reservists, performing artists, and fee-basis government officials. Attach Form 2106 or 2106-EZ — 24
25 IRA deduction (see page 26) — 25
26 Student loan interest deduction (see page 28) — 26
27 Tuition and fees deduction (see page 29) — 27
28 Health savings account deduction. Attach Form 8889 — 28
29 Moving expenses. Attach Form 3903 — 29
30 One-half of self-employment tax. Attach Schedule SE — 30 **2,350.**
31 Self-employed health insurance deduction (see page 30) — 31
32 Self-employed SEP, SIMPLE, and qualified plans — 32
33 Penalty on early withdrawal of savings — 33
34a Alimony paid b Recipient's SSN ▶ — 34a
35 Add lines 23 through 34a — 35 **2,350.**
36 Subtract line 35 from line 22. This is your **adjusted gross income** ▶ — 36 **30,915.**

410001 11-03-04

LHA For Disclosure, Privacy Act, and Paperwork Reduction Act Notice, see page 75.   Form 1040

Example 5:

Form 104C	HARRY JONES	777-88-9999		Page 2

Tax and Credits

37 Amount from line 36 (adjusted gross income) .... **37** 30,915.

Standard Deduction for -

38a Check if: ☐ You were born before January 2, 1940, ☐ Blind. } **Total boxes**
☐ Spouse was born before January 2, 1940, ☐ Blind. } **checked** ► **38a** ☐

● People who checked any box on line 38a or 38b **or** who can be claimed as a dependent.

b If your spouse itemizes on a separate return or you were a dual-status alien, see page 31 and check here ► **38b** ☐

39 **Itemized deductions** (from Schedule A) or your **standard deduction** (see left margin) .... **39** 5,000.

40 Subtract line 39 from line 37 .... **40** 25,915.

41 If line 37 is $107,025 or less, multiply $3,100 by the total number of exemptions claimed on line 6d. If line 37 is over $107,025, see the worksheet on page 33 .... **41** 3,200.

42 **Taxable income**. Subtract line 41 from line 40. If line 41 is more than line 40, enter -0- .... **42** 22,715.

● All others:

43 **Tax**. Check if any tax is from: a ☐ Form(s) 8814 b ☐ Form 4972 .... **43** 3,051.

Single or Married filing separately, $4,850

44 **Alternative minimum tax**. Attach Form 6251 .... **44**

45 Add lines 43 and 44 .... ► **45** 3,051.

Married filing jointly or Qualifying widow(er), $9,700

46 Foreign tax credit. Attach Form 1116 if required **46**
47 Credit for child and dependent care expenses. Attach Form 2441 .... **47**
48 Credit for the elderly or the disabled. Attach Schedule R **48**

Head of household, $7,150

49 Education credits. Attach Form 8863 .... **49**
50 Retirement savings contributions credit. Attach Form 8880 .... **50**
51 Child tax credit (see page 37) **51**
52 Adoption credit. Attach Form 8839 .... **52**
53 Credits from: a ☐ Form 8396 b ☐ Form 8859 .... **53**
54 Other credits. Check applicable box(es): a ☐ Form 3800
b ☐ Form 8801 c ☐ Specify **54**

55 Add lines 46 through 54. These are your **total credits** **55**

56 Subtract line 55 from line 45. If line 55 is more than line 45, enter -0- .... ► **56** 3,051.

Other Taxes

57 Self-employment tax. Attach Schedule SE .... **57** 4,700.
58 Social security and Medicare tax on tip income not reported to employer. Attach Form 4137 .... **58**
59 Additional tax on IRAs, other qualified retirement plans, etc. Attach Form 5329 if required **59**
60 Advance earned income credit payments from Form(s) W-2 .... **60**
61 Household employment taxes. Attach Schedule H **61**
62 Add lines 56 through 61. This is your **total tax** .... ► **62** 7,751.

Payments

63 Federal income tax withheld from Forms W-2 and 1099 .... **63**
64 2004 estimated tax payments and amount applied from 2003 return .... **64** 8,000.
65a **Earned income credit (EIC)** **65a**

If you have a qualifying child, attach Schedule EIC.

b Nontaxable combat pay election ► **65b**
66 Excess social security and tier 1 RRTA tax withheld (see page 54) **66**
67 Additional child tax credit. Attach Form 8812 .... **67**
68 Amount paid with request for extension to file (see page 54) **68**
69 Other payments from: a ☐ Form 2439 b ☐ Form 4136 c ☐ Form 8885 .... **69**
70 Add lines 63, 64, 65a, and 66 through 69. These are your **total payments** .... ► **70** 8,000.

Refund

71 If line 70 is more than line 62, subtract line 62 from line 70. This is the amount you **overpaid** .... **71** 249.

Direct deposit? See page 54 and fill in 72b, 72c, and 72d.

72a Amount of line 71 you want **refunded to you** .... ► **72a** 249.
b Routing number ☐ ► c Type: ☐ Checking ☐ Savings ► d Account number ☐
73 Amount of line 71 you want **applied to your 2005 estimated tax** **73**

Amount You Owe

74 **Amount you owe**. Subtract line 70 from line 62. For details on how to pay, see page 55 .... ► **74**
75 Estimated tax penalty (see page 55) **75**

Third Party Designee

Do you want to allow another person to discuss this return with the IRS (see page 56)? ☐ **Yes**. Complete the following. ☐ **No**
Designee's name ► Phone no. ► Personal identification number (PIN) ►

Sign Here

Under penalties of perjury, I declare that I have examined this return and accompanying schedules and statements, and to the best of my knowledge and belief, they are true, correct, and complete. Declaration of preparer (other than taxpayer) is based on all information of which preparer has any knowledge.

Joint return? See page 17. Keep a copy for your records.

Your signature | Date | Your occupation | Daytime phone number

Spouse's signature. If a joint return, **both** must sign. | Date | Spouse's occupation

Paid Preparer's Use Only

Preparer's signature ► | Date | Check if self-employed ☐ | Preparer's SSN or PTIN

Firm's name (or yours if self-employed), address, and ZIP code ► | EIN | Phone no.

410002 11-03-04

95

How To Turn Your Poker Playing Into A Business

Example 5:

| SCHEDULE C (Form 1040)
Department of the Treasury
Internal Revenue Service | **Profit or Loss From Business**
(Sole Proprietorship)
▶ Partnerships, joint ventures, etc., must file Form 1065 or 1065-B.
▶ Attach to Form 1040 or 1041. ▶See Instructions for Schedule C (Form 1040). | OMB No. 1545-0074
Attachment
Sequence No. **09** |

Name of proprietor	Social security number (SSN)
HARRY JONES	777-88-9999

A	Principal business or profession, including product or service (see page C-2)	B Enter code from pages C-7, 8, & 9
	GAMBLING/WAGERING	▶ 999999

C	Business name. If no separate business name, leave blank.	D Employer ID number (EIN), if any

E Business address (including suite or room no.) ▶ _____
   City, town or post office, state, and ZIP code

F Accounting method: (1) [X] Cash   (2) [ ] Accrual   (3) [ ] Other (specify) ▶ _____

G Did you "materially participate" in the operation of this business during 2004? If "No," see page C-3 for limit on losses   [X] Yes [ ] No

H If you started or acquired this business during 2004, check here   ▶ [ ]

Part I   Income

1	Gross receipts or sales. **Caution.** If this income was reported to you on Form W-2 and the "Statutory employee" box on that form was checked, see page C-3 and check here ▶ [ ]	1	85,000.
2	Returns and allowances	2	
3	Subtract line 2 from line 1	3	85,000.
4	Cost of goods sold (from line 42 on page 2)	4	35,000.
5	**Gross profit.** Subtract line 4 from line 3	5	50,000.
6	Other income, including Federal and state gasoline or fuel tax credit or refund (see page C-3)	6	
7	**Gross income.** Add lines 5 and 6 ▶	7	50,000.

Part II   Expenses. Enter expenses for business use of your home **only** on line 30.

8	Advertising	8		19	Pension and profit-sharing plans	19	
9	Car and truck expenses (see page C-3)	9	3,600.	20	Rent or lease (see page C-5):		
				a	Vehicles, machinery, and equipment	20a	
10	Commissions and fees	10		b	Other business property	20b	
11	Contract labor (see page C-4)	11		21	Repairs and maintenance	21	
12	Depletion	12		22	Supplies (not included in Part III)	22	
13	Depreciation and section 179 expense deduction (not included in Part III) (see page C-4)	13		23	Taxes and licenses	23	75.
				24	Travel, meals, and entertainment:		
14	Employee benefit programs (other than on line 19)	14		a	Travel	24a	8,000.
15	Insurance (other than health)	15		b	Meals and entertainment 4,000.		
16	Interest:			c	Enter nondeductible amount included on line 24b (see page C-5) 2,000.		
a	Mortgage (paid to banks, etc.)	16a		d	Subtract line 24c from line 24b	24d	2,000.
b	Other	16b		25	Utilities	25	
17	Legal and professional services	17	350.	26	Wages (less employment credits)	26	
18	Office expense	18	275.	27	Other expenses (from line 48 on page 2)	27	2,435.

28	**Total expenses** before expenses for business use of home. Add lines 8 through 27 in columns ▶	28	16,735.
29	Tentative profit (loss). Subtract line 28 from line 7	29	33,265.
30	Expenses for business use of your home. Attach Form 8829	30	
31	**Net profit or (loss).** Subtract line 30 from line 29. • If a profit, enter on **Form 1040, line 12,** and **also** on **Schedule SE, line 2** (statutory employees, see page C-6). Estates and trusts, enter on Form 1041, line 3. • If a loss, you **must** go to line 32.	31	33,265.
32	If you have a loss, check the box that describes your investment in this activity (see page C-6). • If you checked 32a, enter the loss on **Form 1040, line 12,** and **also** on **Schedule SE, line 2** (statutory employees, see page C-6). Estates and trusts, enter on Form 1041, line 3. • If you checked 32b, you **must** attach Form 6198.	32a [ ] All investment is at risk. 32b [ ] Some investment is not at risk.

LHA   **For Paperwork Reduction Act Notice, see Form 1040 instructions.**   Schedule C (Form 1040)
420001 11-03-04

Example 5:

Schedule C (Form 1040) 2004 HARRY JONES		777-88-9999 Page 2

Part III | Cost of Goods Sold (see page C-6)

33   Method(s) used to
value closing inventory: **a** ☐ Cost   **b** ☐ Lower of cost or market   **c** ☐ Other (attach explanation)

34   Was there any change in determining quantities, costs, or valuations between opening and closing inventory? If
"Yes," attach explanation .... ☐ Yes   ☐ No

35	Inventory at beginning of year. If different from last year's closing inventory, attach explanation	35	
36	Purchases less cost of items withdrawn for personal use	36	
37	Cost of labor. Do not include any amounts paid to yourself	37	
38	Materials and supplies	38	
39	Other costs	39	35,000.
40	Add lines 35 through 39	40	35,000.
41	Inventory at end of year	41	
42	**Cost of goods sold.** Subtract line 41 from line 40. Enter the result here and on page 1, line 4	42	35,000.

Part IV | Information on Your Vehicle. Complete this part **only** if you are claiming car or truck expenses on line 9 and are not required to file Form 4562 for this business. See the instructions for line 13 on page C-4 to find out if you must file Form 4562.

43   When did you place your vehicle in service for business purposes? (month, day, year)   ▶   01 / 01 / 04 .

44   Of the total number of miles you drove your vehicle during 2004, enter the number of miles you used your vehicle for:
   a Business   9,600   **b** Commuting _____   **c** Other   5,400

45   Do you (or your spouse) have another vehicle available for personal use? .... ☒ Yes   ☐ No

46   Was your vehicle available for personal use during off-duty hours? .... ☒ Yes   ☐ No

47 **a** Do you have evidence to support your deduction? .... ☒ Yes   ☐ No
   b If "Yes," is the evidence written? .... ☒ Yes   ☐ No

Part V | Other Expenses. List below business expenses not included on lines 8-26 or line 30.

BANK CHARGES	60.
BOOKS	250.
BANK CHARGES	25.
CELL PHONE	1,500.
INTERNET FEES	600.
48 **Total other expenses.** Enter here and on page 1, line 27	2,435.

420002/ 11-03-04   Schedule C (Form 1040) 2004

How To Turn Your Poker Playing Into A Business

Example 5:

Name of person with **self-employment** income (as shown on Form 1040)

HARRY JONES

Social security number of person with **self-employment** income .... ▶ | 777 : 88 : 9999

Who Must File Schedule SE

You must file Schedule SE if:

- You had net earnings from self-employment from **other than** church employee income (line 4 of Short Schedule SE or line 4c of Long Schedule SE) of $400 or more **or**

- You had church employee income of $108.28 or more. Income from services you performed as a minister or a member of a religious order **is not** church employee income (see page SE-1).

Note. Even if you had a loss or a small amount of income from self-employment, it may be to your benefit to file Schedule SE and use either "optional method" in Part II of Long Schedule SE (see page SE-3).

Exception. If your only self-employment income was from earnings as a minister, member of a religious order, or Christian Science practitioner **and** you filed Form 4361 and received IRS approval not to be taxed on those earnings, **do not** file Schedule SE. Instead, write "Exempt-Form 4361" on Form 1040, line 57.

May I Use Short Schedule SE or Must I Use Long Schedule SE?

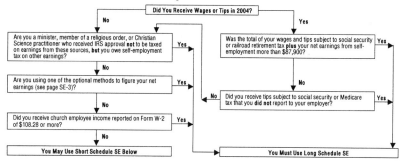

Section A-Short Schedule SE. Caution. Read above to see if you can use Short Schedule SE.

1 Net farm profit or (loss) from Schedule F, line 36, and farm partnerships, Schedule K-1 (Form 1065), box 14, code A	**1**	
2 Net profit or (loss) from Schedule C, line 31; Schedule C-EZ, line 3; Schedule K-1 (Form 1065), box 14, code A (other than farming); and Schedule K-1 (Form 1065-B), box 9. Ministers and members of religious orders, see page SE-1 for amounts to report on this line. See page SE-2 for other income to report	**2**	33,265.
3 Combine lines 1 and 2	**3**	33,265.
4 **Net earnings from self-employment.** Multiply line 3 by 92.35% (.9235). If less than $400, **do not** file this schedule; you do not owe self-employment tax .... ▶	**4**	30,720.
5 **Self-employment tax.** If the amount on line 4 is: • $87,900 or less, multiply line 4 by 15.3% (.153). Enter the result here and on **Form 1040, line 57.** • More than $87,900, multiply line 4 by 2.9% (.029). Then, add $10,899.60 to the result. Enter the total here and on **Form 1040, line 57.**	**5**	4,700.
6 **Deduction for one-half of self-employment tax.** Multiply line 5 by 50% (.5). Enter the result here and on **Form 1040, line 30**	**6**	2,350.

LHA   For Paperwork Reduction Act Notice, see Form 1040 instructions.

Schedule SE (Form 1040) 2004

424501
10-27-04

98

NOTES TO EXAMPLE 5

Harry ends up with a profit from his business of $33,265 after all of his expenses. Notice that the Meals and Entertainment are limited to 50%. Also, notice that the IRS allows you to take ½ of your Self-Employment tax as a deduction on the front of the return as an adjustment. Here Harry ends up with a refund of $249

EXAMPLE 6- BUSINESS TAX RETURN WITH RETIREMENT PLAN

Let's use the same facts in Example 5, except that Harry wants to maximize his Self-Employed Pension Plan (SEP). His profit from his Schedule C is the same as in Example 5 but he can now take his SEP as an adjustment on the front of his tax return to reduce his Adjusted Gross Income (AGI).

The amount he can put into his SEP is $6,183. This is calculated by taking his profit of $33,265, subtracting out ½ of his Self-Employment Tax of $2,350 and then multiplying this by 20%. Harry now has a refund of $1,179.

How To Turn Your Poker Playing Into A Business

Example 6:

Form **1040** U.S. Individual Income Tax Return (99) IRS Use Only - Do not write or staple in this space.

Label (See instructions on page 16.) Use the IRS label. Otherwise, please print or type.

For the year Jan. 1-Dec. 31, or other tax year beginning , ending 20 | OMB No. 1545-0074

Your first name and initial: **HARRY** — Last name: **JONES** — Your social security number: **777 88 9999**

If a joint return, spouse's first name and initial — Last name — Spouse's social security number

Home address (number and street). If you have a P.O. box, see page 16. **4444 QUAD COURT** Apt. no.

City, town or post office, state, and ZIP code. If you have a foreign address, see page 16. **RAINBOW, GA 99888**

▲ **Important!** ▲ You **must** enter your SSN(s) above.

Presidential Election Campaign (See page 16.) ► Note. Checking "Yes" will not change your tax or reduce your refund. Do you, or your spouse if filing a joint return, want $3 to go to this fund? ► You: ☐ Yes ☒ No Spouse: ☐ Yes ☐ No

Filing Status — Check only one box.
1 ☒ Single
2 ☐ Married filing jointly (even if only one had income)
3 ☐ Married filing separately. Enter spouse's SSN above and full name here. ►
4 ☐ Head of household (with qualifying person). (See page 17.) If the qualifying person is a child but not your dependent, enter this child's name here. ►
5 ☐ Qualifying widow(er) with dependent child (see page 17)

Exemptions
6a ☒ Yourself. If someone can claim you as a dependent, **do not** check box 6a
b ☐ Spouse
c Dependents:
(1) First name / Last name / (2) Dependent's social security number / (3) Dependent's relationship to you / (4) ✓ if qualifying child for child tax credit (see page 18)

Boxes checked on 6a and 6b: **1**
No. of children on 6c who: ● lived with you ● did not live with you due to divorce or separation (see page 18)
Dependents on 6c not entered above
Add numbers on lines above ► **1**

If more than four dependents, see page 18.
d Total number of exemptions claimed

Income
Attach Form(s) W-2 here. Also attach Forms W-2G and 1099-R if tax was withheld.
7 Wages, salaries, tips, etc. Attach Form(s) W-2 | 7
8a Taxable interest. Attach Schedule B if required | 8a
b Tax-exempt interest. Do not include on line 8a | 8b
9a Ordinary dividends. Attach Schedule B if required | 9a
b Qualified dividends (see page 20) | 9b
10 Taxable refunds, credits, or offsets of state and local income taxes | 10
11 Alimony received | 11
12 Business income or (loss). Attach Schedule C or C-EZ | 12 | **33,265.**
13 Capital gain or (loss). Attach Schedule D if required. If not required, check here ► ☐ | 13
14 Other gains or (losses). Attach Form 4797 | 14
15a IRA distributions | 15a | b Taxable amount (see page 22) | 15b
16a Pensions and annuities | 16a | b Taxable amount (see page 22) | 16b
17 Rental real estate, royalties, partnerships, S corporations, trusts, etc. Attach Schedule E | 17
18 Farm income or (loss). Attach Schedule F | 18
19 Unemployment compensation | 19
20a Social security benefits | 20a | b Taxable amount (see page 24) | 20b
21 Other income. List type and amount (see page 24) | 21
22 Add the amounts in the far right column for lines 7 through 21. This is your **total income** ► | 22 | **33,265.**

If you did not get a W-2, see page 19.
Enclose, but do not attach, any payment. Also, please use Form 1040-V.

Adjusted Gross Income
23 Educator expenses (see page 26) | 23
24 Certain business expenses of reservists, performing artists, and fee-basis government officials. Attach Form 2106 or 2106-EZ | 24
25 IRA deduction (see page 26) | 25
26 Student loan interest deduction (see page 28) | 26
27 Tuition and fees deduction (see page 29) | 27
28 Health savings account deduction. Attach Form 8889 | 28
29 Moving expenses. Attach Form 3903 | 29
30 One-half of self-employment tax. Attach Schedule SE | 30 | **2,350.**
31 Self-employed health insurance deduction (see page 30) | 31
32 Self-employed SEP, SIMPLE, and qualified plans | 32 | **6,183.**
33 Penalty on early withdrawal of savings | 33
34a Alimony paid b Recipient's SSN ► | 34a
35 Add lines 23 through 34a | 35 | **8,533.**
36 Subtract line 35 from line 22. This is your **adjusted gross income** ► | 36 | **24,732.**

410001 11-03-04
LHA For Disclosure, Privacy Act, and Paperwork Reduction Act Notice, see page 75. Form **1040**

100

Example 6:

Form 104C	HARRY JONES	777-88-9999		Page 2

Tax and Credits	37	Amount from line 36 (adjusted gross income)		37	24,732.
Standard Deduction for -	38a	Check ⎧ ☐ **You** were born before January 2, 1940, ☐ Blind. ⎫ **Total boxes** ⎩ **if:** ☐ **Spouse** was born before January 2, 1940, ☐ Blind. ⎭ checked ▶ 38a			
● People who checked any box on line 38a or 38b **or** who can be claimed as a dependent.	b	If your spouse itemizes on a separate return or you were a dual-status alien, see page 31 and check here ▶ 38b ☐			
	39	**Itemized deductions** (from Schedule A) **or your standard deduction** (see left margin)		39	5,000.
	40	Subtract line 39 from line 37		40	19,732.
	41	If line 37 is $107,025 or less, multiply $3,100 by the total number of exemptions claimed on line 6d. If line 37 is over $107,025, see the worksheet on page 33		41	3,200.
● All others:	42	**Taxable income.** Subtract line 41 from line 40. If line 41 is more than line 40, enter -0-		42	16,532.
Single or Married filing separately, $4,850	43	**Tax.** Check if any tax is from: **a** ☐ Form(s) 8814 **b** ☐ Form 4972		43	2,121.
	44	**Alternative minimum tax.** Attach Form 6251		44	
Married filing jointly or Qualifying widow(er), $9,700	45	Add lines 43 and 44 ▶		45	2,121.
	46	Foreign tax credit. Attach Form 1116 if required	46		
	47	Credit for child and dependent care expenses. Attach Form 2441	47		
Head of household, $7,150	48	Credit for the elderly or the disabled. Attach Schedule R	48		
	49	Education credits. Attach Form 8863	49		
	50	Retirement savings contributions credit. Attach Form 8880	50		
	51	Child tax credit (see page 37)	51		
	52	Adoption credit. Attach Form 8839	52		
	53	Credits from: **a** ☐ Form 8396 **b** ☐ Form 8859	53		
	54	Other credits. Check applicable box(es): **a** ☐ Form 3800 **b** ☐ Form 8801 **c** ☐ Specify	54		
	55	Add lines 46 through 54. These are your **total credits**		55	
	56	Subtract line 55 from line 45. If line 55 is more than line 45, enter -0- ▶		56	2,121.
Other Taxes	57	Self-employment tax. Attach Schedule SE		57	4,700.
	58	Social security and Medicare tax on tip income not reported to employer. Attach Form 4137		58	
	59	Additional tax on IRAs, other qualified retirement plans, etc. Attach Form 5329 if required		59	
	60	Advance earned income credit payments from Form(s) W-2		60	
	61	Household employment taxes. Attach Schedule H		61	
	62	Add lines 56 through 61. This is your **total tax** ▶		62	6,821.
Payments	63	Federal income tax withheld from Forms W-2 and 1099	63		
	64	2004 estimated tax payments and amount applied from 2003 return	64	8,000.	
If you have a qualifying child, attach Schedule EIC.	65a	**Earned income credit (EIC)**	65a		
	b	Nontaxable combat pay election ▶	65b		
	66	Excess social security and tier 1 RRTA tax withheld (see page 54)	66		
	67	Additional child tax credit. Attach Form 8812	67		
	68	Amount paid with request for extension to file (see page 54)	68		
	69	Other payments from: **a** ☐ Form 2439 **b** ☐ Form 4136 **c** ☐ Form 8885	69		
	70	Add lines 63, 64, 65a, and 66 through 69. These are your **total payments** ▶		70	8,000.
Refund	71	If line 70 is more than line 62, subtract line 62 from line 70. This is the amount you **overpaid**		71	1,179.
Direct deposit? See page 54 and fill in 72b, 72c, and 72d.	72a	Amount of line 71 you want **refunded to you** ▶		72a	1,179.
	b	Routing number ▶ **c** Type: ☐ Checking ☐ Savings **d** Account number ▶			
	73	Amount of line 71 you want **applied to your 2005 estimated tax** ▶	73		
Amount You Owe	74	**Amount you owe.** Subtract line 70 from line 62. For details on how to pay, see page 55 ▶		74	
	75	Estimated tax penalty (see page 55)	75		
Third Party Designee		Do you want to allow another person to discuss this return with the IRS (see page 56)? ☐ **Yes.** Complete the following. ☐ **No** Designee's ▶ name Phone no. ▶ Personal identification number (PIN) ▶			
Sign Here		Under penalties of perjury, I declare that I have examined this return and accompanying schedules and statements, and to the best of my knowledge and belief, they are true, correct, and complete. Declaration of preparer (other than taxpayer) is based on all information of which preparer has any knowledge.			
Joint return? See page 17. Keep a copy for your records.		Your signature ▶ Date Your occupation Daytime phone number			
		Spouse's signature. If a joint return, **both** must sign. ▶ Date Spouse's occupation			
Paid Preparer's Use Only		Preparer's signature ▶ Date Check if self-employed ☐ Preparer's SSN or PTIN			
410002 11-03-04		Firm's name (or yours if self-employed), address, and ZIP code ▶ EIN Phone no.			

How To Turn Your Poker Playing Into A Business

Example 6:

SCHEDULE C
(Form 1040)

Department of the Treasury
Internal Revenue Service

Profit or Loss From Business
(Sole Proprietorship)

▶ Partnerships, joint ventures, etc., must file Form 1065 or 1065-B.
▶ Attach to Form 1040 or 1041. ▶ See Instructions for Schedule C (Form 1040).

Attachment
Sequence No. **09**

Name of proprietor: **HARRY JONES**

Social security number (SSN): **777-88-9999**

A Principal business or profession, including product or service (see page C-2)
GAMBLING/WAGERING

B Enter code from pages C-7, 8, & 9
▶ **999999**

C Business name. If no separate business name, leave blank.

D Employer ID number (EIN), if any

E Business address (including suite or room no.) ▶
City, town or post office, state, and ZIP code

F Accounting method: (1) [X] Cash (2) [ ] Accrual (3) [ ] Other (specify) ▶

G Did you "materially participate" in the operation of this business during 2004? If "No," see page C-3 for limit on losses ... [X] Yes [ ] No

H If you started or acquired this business during 2004, check here ... ▶ [ ]

Part I — Income

1	Gross receipts or sales. **Caution.** If this income was reported to you on Form W-2 and the "Statutory employee" box on that form was checked, see page C-3 and check here ... ▶ [ ] **1**	85,000.
2	Returns and allowances **2**	
3	Subtract line 2 from line 1 **3**	85,000.
4	Cost of goods sold (from line 42 on page 2) **4**	35,000.
5	**Gross profit.** Subtract line 4 from line 3 **5**	50,000.
6	Other income, including Federal and state gasoline or fuel tax credit or refund (see page C-3) **6**	
7	**Gross income.** Add lines 5 and 6 ... ▶ **7**	50,000.

Part II — Expenses. Enter expenses for business use of your home **only** on line 30.

8	Advertising	**8**		19	Pension and profit-sharing plans **19**	
9	Car and truck expenses (see page C-3) Stmt. 2	**9**	3,600.	20	Rent or lease (see page C-5):	
10	Commissions and fees	**10**		a	Vehicles, machinery, and equipment **20a**	
11	Contract labor (see page C-4)	**11**		b	Other business property **20b**	
12	Depletion	**12**		21	Repairs and maintenance **21**	
13	Depreciation and section 179 expense deduction (not included in Part III) (see page C-4)	**13**		22	Supplies (not included in Part III) **22**	
				23	Taxes and licenses **23**	75.
14	Employee benefit programs (other than on line 19)	**14**		24	Travel, meals, and entertainment:	
15	Insurance (other than health)	**15**		a	Travel **24a**	8,000.
16	Interest:			b	Meals and entertainment 4,000.	
a	Mortgage (paid to banks, etc.)	**16a**		c	Enter nondeductible amount included on line 24b (see page C-5) 2,000.	
b	Other	**16b**		d	Subtract line 24c from line 24b **24d**	2,000.
17	Legal and professional services	**17**	350.	25	Utilities **25**	
18	Office expense	**18**	275.	26	Wages (less employment credits) **26**	
				27	Other expenses (from line 48 on page 2) **27**	2,435.
28	**Total expenses** before expenses for business use of home. Add lines 8 through 27 in columns ... ▶ **28**					16,735.

29	Tentative profit (loss). Subtract line 28 from line 7 **29**	33,265.
30	Expenses for business use of your home. Attach Form 8829 **30**	
31	**Net profit or (loss).** Subtract line 30 from line 29.	
	• If a profit, enter on **Form 1040, line 12,** and **also on Schedule SE, line 2** (statutory employees, see page C-6). Estates and trusts, enter on Form 1041, line 3.	
	• If a loss, you **must** go to line 32. **31**	33,265.
32	If you have a loss, check the box that describes your investment in this activity (see page C-6).	
	• If you checked 32a, enter the loss on **Form 1040, line 12,** and **also on Schedule SE, line 2** (statutory employees, see page C-6). Estates and trusts, enter on Form 1041, line 3.	
	• If you checked 32b, you **must** attach Form 6198.	32a [ ] All investment is at risk. 32b [ ] Some investment is not at risk.

LHA For Paperwork Reduction Act Notice, see Form 1040 instructions.

420001 11-03-04

Schedule C (Form 1040)

Example 6:

Schedule C (Form 1040)   **HARRY JONES**   777-88-9999 Page **2**

Part III | Cost of Goods Sold (see page C-6)

33   Method(s) used to value closing inventory: **a** ☐ Cost   **b** ☐ Lower of cost or market   **c** ☐ Other (attach explanation)

34   Was there any change in determining quantities, costs, or valuations between opening and closing inventory? If "Yes," attach explanation   ☐ Yes ☐ No

35	Inventory at beginning of year. If different from last year's closing inventory, attach explanation	35	
36	Purchases less cost of items withdrawn for personal use	36	
37	Cost of labor. Do not include any amounts paid to yourself	37	
38	Materials and supplies	38	
39	Other costs See Statement 3	39	35,000.
40	Add lines 35 through 39	40	35,000.
41	Inventory at end of year	41	
42	**Cost of goods sold.** Subtract line 41 from line 40. Enter the result here and on page 1, line 4	42	35,000.

Part IV | Information on Your Vehicle. Complete this part **only** if you are claiming car or truck expenses on line 9 and are not required to file Form 4562 for this business. See the instructions for line 13 on page C-4 to find out if you must file Form 4562.

43   When did you place your vehicle in service for business purposes? (month, day, year)   ▶ 01/01/04.

44   Of the total number of miles you drove your vehicle during 2004, enter the number of miles you used your vehicle for:

   a Business   9,600   **b** Commuting   **c** Other   5,400

45   Do you (or your spouse) have another vehicle available for personal use?   ☒ Yes ☐ No

46   Was your vehicle available for personal use during off-duty hours?   ☒ Yes ☐ No

47 **a** Do you have evidence to support your deduction?   ☒ Yes ☐ No
   b If "Yes," is the evidence written?   ☒ Yes ☐ No

Part V | Other Expenses. List below business expenses not included on lines 8-26 or line 30.

BANK CHARGES	60.
BOOKS	250.
BANK CHARGES	25.
CELL PHONE	1,500.
INTERNET FEES	600.
48 Total other expenses. Enter here and on page 1, line 27 48	2,435.

420002/ 11-03-04   Schedule C (Form 1040)

103

How To Turn Your Poker Playing Into A Business

Example 6:

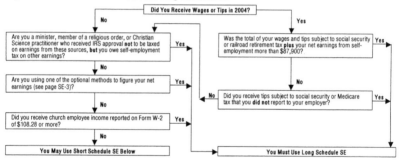

SCHEDULE SE
(Form 1040)

Department of the Treasury
Internal Revenue Service

Self-Employment Tax

▶ Attach to Form 1040. ▶ See Instructions for Schedule SE (Form 1040).

OMB No. 1545-0074

Attachment
Sequence No. **17**

Name of person with **self-employment** income (as shown on Form 1040)

HARRY JONES

Social security number of
person with **self-employment**
income ▶ | 777 | 88 | 9999

Who Must File Schedule SE

You must file Schedule SE if:

- You had net earnings from self-employment from **other than** church employee income (line 4 of Short Schedule SE or line 4c of Long Schedule SE) of $400 or more **or**
- You had church employee income of $108.28 or more. Income from services you performed as a minister or a member of a religious order **is not** church employee income (see page SE-1).

Note. Even if you had a loss or a small amount of income from self-employment, it may be to your benefit to file Schedule SE and use either "optional method" in Part II of Long Schedule SE (see page SE-3).

Exception. If your only self-employment income was from earnings as a minister, member of a religious order, or Christian Science practitioner **and** you filed Form 4361 and received IRS approval not to be taxed on those earnings, **do not** file Schedule SE. Instead, write "Exempt-Form 4361" on Form 1040, line 57.

May I Use Short Schedule SE or Must I Use Long Schedule SE?

```
                    ┌── Did You Receive Wages or Tips in 2004? ──┐
              No                                                    Yes
```

Are you a minister, member of a religious order, or Christian Science practitioner who received IRS approval **not** to be taxed on earnings from these sources, **but** you owe self-employment tax on other earnings? → **Yes**

Was the total of your wages and tips subject to social security or railroad retirement tax **plus** your net earnings from self-employment more than $87,900? → **Yes**

↓ **No**

Are you using one of the optional methods to figure your net earnings (see page SE-3)? → **Yes**

No

Did you receive tips subject to social security or Medicare tax that you **did not** report to your employer? → **Yes**

↓ **No**

← **No**

Did you receive church employee income reported on Form W-2 of $108.28 or more? → **Yes**

↓ **No**

You May Use Short Schedule SE Below

You Must Use Long Schedule SE

Section A-Short Schedule SE. Caution. Read above to see if you can use Short Schedule SE.

1 Net farm profit or (loss) from Schedule F, line 36, and farm partnerships, Schedule K-1 (Form 1065), box 14, code A	**1**	
2 Net profit or (loss) from Schedule C, line 31; Schedule C-EZ, line 3; Schedule K-1 (Form 1065), box 14, code A (other than farming); and Schedule K-1 (Form 1065-B), box 9. Ministers and members of religious orders, see page SE-1 for amounts to report on this line. See page SE-2 for other income to report **Stmt 4**	**2**	33,265.
3 Combine lines 1 and 2	**3**	33,265.
4 **Net earnings from self-employment.** Multiply line 3 by 92.35% (.9235). If less than $400, **do not** file this schedule; you do not owe self-employment tax ▶	**4**	30,720.
5 **Self-employment tax.** If the amount on line 4 is: • $87,900 or less, multiply line 4 by 15.3% (.153). Enter the result here and on **Form 1040, line 57.** • More than $87,900, multiply line 4 by 2.9% (.029). Then, add $10,899.60 to the result. Enter the total here and on **Form 1040, line 57.**	**5**	4,700.
6 Deduction for one-half of self-employment tax. Multiply line 5 by 50% (.5). Enter the result here and on **Form 1040, line 30** **6**	2,350.	

LHA   For Paperwork Reduction Act Notice, see Form 1040 instructions.

Schedule SE (Form 1040)

424501
10-27-04

EXAMPLE 7- BUSINESS TAX RETURN WITH RETIREMENT PLAN AND HEALTH INSURANCE

Let's now use Example 5, with maximizing a SEP plan as in Example 6. In this example, Harry has paid $9,600 out of pocket for Health insurance.

The total income is the same but now the AGI has changed. The amount Harry paid for Health insurance can be deducted on the front page of his tax return because he is self-employed and he made a profit of at least as much as the cost of the insurance. He now has a refund of $2,607.

Example 7:

Form **1040**	U.S. Individual Income Tax Return		(99)	IRS Use Only - Do not write or staple in this space.		

For the year Jan. 1-Dec. 31, , or other tax year beginning , ending , 20   OMB No. 1545-0074

Label
(See instructions on page 16.)

Use the IRS label. Otherwise, please print or type.

L A B E L
H E R E

Your first name and initial: **HARRY**   Last name: **JONES**   Your social security number: **777 88 9999**

If a joint return, spouse's first name and initial   Last name   Spouse's social security number

Home address (number and street). If you have a P.O. box, see page 16.   Apt. no.
4444 QUAD COURT

City, town or post office, state, and ZIP code. If you have a foreign address, see page 16.
RAINBOW, GA 99888

▲ **Important!** ▲
You **must** enter your SSN(s) above.

Presidential Election Campaign
(See page 16.) ▶ Note. Checking "Yes" will not change your tax or reduce your refund.
Do you, or your spouse if filing a joint return, want $3 to go to this fund? ▶ **You** Yes [ ] [X] No **Spouse** Yes [ ] [ ] No

Filing Status

Check only one box.

1 [X] Single
2 [ ] Married filing jointly (even if only one had income)
3 [ ] Married filing separately. Enter spouse's SSN above and full name here. ▶
4 [ ] Head of household (with qualifying person). (See page 17.) If the qualifying person is a child but not your dependent, enter this child's name here. ▶
5 [ ] Qualifying widow(er) with dependent child (see page 17)

Exemptions

6a [X] Yourself. If someone can claim you as a dependent, **do not** check box 6a
b [ ] Spouse

Boxes checked on 6a and 6b: **1**
No. of children on 6c who:

c Dependents:

(1) First name Last name	(2) Dependent's social security number	(3) Dependent's relationship to you	(4) ✓ if qualifying child for child tax credit (see page 18)

If more than four dependents, see page 18.

• lived with you
• did not live with you due to divorce or separation (see page 18)

Dependents on 6c not entered above

d Total number of exemptions claimed

Add numbers on lines above ▶ **1**

Income

Attach Form(s) W-2 here. Also attach Forms W-2G and 1099-R if tax was withheld.

If you did not get a W-2, see page 19.

Enclose, but do not attach, any payment. Also, please use Form 1040-V.

7	Wages, salaries, tips, etc. Attach Form(s) W-2		7	
8a	Taxable interest. Attach Schedule B if required		8a	
b	Tax-exempt interest. Do **not** include on line 8a	8b		
9a	Ordinary dividends. Attach Schedule B if required		9a	
b	Qualified dividends (see page 20)	9b		
10	Taxable refunds, credits, or offsets of state and local income taxes		10	
11	Alimony received		11	
12	Business income or (loss). Attach Schedule C or C-EZ		12	33,265.
13	Capital gain or (loss). Attach Schedule D if required. If not required, check here ▶ [ ]		13	
14	Other gains or (losses). Attach Form 4797		14	
15a	IRA distributions	15a	b Taxable amount (see page 22)	15b	
16a	Pensions and annuities	16a	b Taxable amount (see page 22)	16b	
17	Rental real estate, royalties, partnerships, S corporations, trusts, etc. Attach Schedule E		17	
18	Farm income or (loss). Attach Schedule F		18	
19	Unemployment compensation		19	
20a	Social security benefits	20a	b Taxable amount (see page 24)	20b	
21	Other income. List type and amount (see page 24)		21	
22	Add the amounts in the far right column for lines 7 through 21. This is your **total income** ▶		22	33,265.

Adjusted Gross Income

23	Educator expenses (see page 26)	23		
24	Certain business expenses of reservists, performing artists, and fee-basis government officials. Attach Form 2106 or 2106-EZ	24		
25	IRA deduction (see page 26)	25		
26	Student loan interest deduction (see page 28)	26		
27	Tuition and fees deduction (see page 29)	27		
28	Health savings account deduction. Attach Form 8889	28		
29	Moving expenses. Attach Form 3903	29		
30	One-half of self-employment tax. Attach Schedule SE	30	2,350.	
31	Self-employed health insurance deduction (see page 30)	31	9,600.	
32	Self-employed SEP, SIMPLE, and qualified plans	32	6,183.	
33	Penalty on early withdrawal of savings	33		
34a	Alimony paid b Recipient's SSN ▶	34a		
35	Add lines 23 through 34a		35	18,133.
36	Subtract line 35 from line 22. This is your **adjusted gross income** ▶		36	15,132.

410001 11-03-04

LHA For Disclosure, Privacy Act, and Paperwork Reduction Act Notice, see page 75.   Form **1040**

Example 7:

Form 1040	HARRY JONES	777-88-9999		Page 2

Tax and Credits

Standard Deduction for -
● People who checked any box on line 38a or 38b **or** who can be claimed as a dependent.
● All others:
Single or Married filing separately, $4,850
Married filing jointly or Qualifying widow(er), $9,700
Head of household, $7,150

37	Amount from line 36 (adjusted gross income)	37	15,132.
38a	Check if: ☐ You were born before January 2, 1940, ☐ Blind. ☐ Spouse was born before January 2, 1940, ☐ Blind. } Total boxes checked ▶ 38a		
b	If your spouse itemizes on a separate return or you were a dual-status alien, see page 31 and check here ▶ 38b ☐		
39	Itemized deductions (from Schedule A) or your standard deduction (see left margin)	39	5,000.
40	Subtract line 39 from line 37	40	10,132.
41	If line 37 is $107,025 or less, multiply $3,100 by the total number of exemptions claimed on line 6d. If line 37 is over $107,025, see the worksheet on page 33	41	3,200.
42	Taxable income. Subtract line 41 from line 40. If line 41 is more than line 40, enter -0-	42	6,932.
43	Tax. Check if any tax is from: a ☐ Form(s) 8814 b ☐ Form 4972	43	693.
44	Alternative minimum tax. Attach Form 6251	44	
45	Add lines 43 and 44 ▶	45	693.
46	Foreign tax credit. Attach Form 1116 if required ... 46		
47	Credit for child and dependent care expenses. Attach Form 2441 ... 47		
48	Credit for the elderly or the disabled. Attach Schedule R ... 48		
49	Education credits. Attach Form 8863 ... 49		
50	Retirement savings contributions credit. Attach Form 8880 ... 50		
51	Child tax credit (see page 37) ... 51		
52	Adoption credit. Attach Form 8839 ... 52		
53	Credits from: a ☐ Form 8396 b ☐ Form 8859 ... 53		
54	Other credits. Check applicable box(es): a ☐ Form 3800 b ☐ Form 8801 c ☐ Specify ___ 54		
55	Add lines 46 through 54. These are your total credits	55	
56	Subtract line 55 from line 45. If line 55 is more than line 45, enter -0- ▶	56	693.

Other Taxes

57	Self-employment tax. Attach Schedule SE	57	4,700.
58	Social security and Medicare tax on tip income not reported to employer. Attach Form 4137	58	
59	Additional tax on IRAs, other qualified retirement plans, etc. Attach Form 5329 if required	59	
60	Advance earned income credit payments from Form(s) W-2	60	
61	Household employment taxes. Attach Schedule H	61	
62	Add lines 56 through 61. This is your total tax ▶	62	5,393.

Payments

If you have a qualifying child, attach Schedule EIC.

63	Federal income tax withheld from Forms W-2 and 1099 ... 63		
64	2004 estimated tax payments and amount applied from 2003 return ... 64	8,000.	
65a	Earned income credit (EIC) ... 65a		
b	Nontaxable combat pay election ▶ 65b		
66	Excess social security and tier 1 RRTA tax withheld (see page 54) ... 66		
67	Additional child tax credit. Attach Form 8812 ... 67		
68	Amount paid with request for extension to file (see page 54) ... 68		
69	Other payments from: a ☐ Form 2439 b ☐ Form 4136 c ☐ Form 8885 ... 69		
70	Add lines 63, 64, 65a, and 66 through 69. These are your total payments ▶	70	8,000.

Refund

Direct deposit? See page 54 and fill in 72b, 72c, and 72d.

71	If line 70 is more than line 62, subtract line 62 from line 70. This is the amount you overpaid	71	2,607.
72a	Amount of line 71 you want refunded to you ▶	72a	2,607.
b	Routing number	c Type: ☐ Checking ☐ Savings ▶ d Account number	
73	Amount of line 71 you want applied to your 2005 estimated tax ▶ 73		

Amount You Owe

74	Amount you owe. Subtract line 70 from line 62. For details on how to pay, see page 55 ▶	74	
75	Estimated tax penalty (see page 55) ... 75		

Third Party Designee Do you want to allow another person to discuss this return with the IRS (see page 56)? ☐ Yes. Complete the following. ☐ No
Designee's name ▶ Phone no. ▶ Personal identification number (PIN) ▶

Sign Here
Joint return? See page 17. Keep a copy for your records.
Under penalties of perjury, I declare that I have examined this return and accompanying schedules and statements, and to the best of my knowledge and belief, they are true, correct, and complete. Declaration of preparer (other than taxpayer) is based on all information of which preparer has any knowledge.
Your signature | Date | Your occupation | Daytime phone number
Spouse's signature. If a joint return, both must sign. | Date | Spouse's occupation

Paid Preparer's Use Only
Preparer's signature ▶ | Date | Check if self-employed ☐ | Preparer's SSN or PTIN
Firm's name (or yours if self-employed), address, and ZIP code ▶ | | EIN | Phone no.

410002 11-03-04

Example 7:

SCHEDULE C (Form 1040)	**Profit or Loss From Business**	OMB No. 1545-0074
Department of the Treasury Internal Revenue Service	(Sole Proprietorship) ▶ Partnerships, joint ventures, etc., must file Form 1065 or 1065-B. ▶ Attach to Form 1040 or 1041. ▶ See Instructions for Schedule C (Form 1040).	Attachment Sequence No. 09

Name of proprietor	Social security number (SSN)
HARRY JONES	777-88-9999

A	Principal business or profession, including product or service (see page C-2)	B Enter code from pages C-7, 8, & 9
	GAMBLING/WAGERING	▶ 999999
C	Business name. If no separate business name, leave blank.	D Employer ID number (EIN), if any

E   Business address (including suite or room no.) ▶ _____
    City, town or post office, state, and ZIP code

F   Accounting method: (1) [X] Cash   (2) [ ] Accrual   (3) [ ] Other (specify) ▶ _____

G   Did you "materially participate" in the operation of this business during 2004? If "No," see page C-3 for limit on losses   [X] Yes [ ] No

H   If you started or acquired this business during 2004, check here   ▶ [ ]

Part I   Income

1	Gross receipts or sales. **Caution.** If this income was reported to you on Form W-2 and the "Statutory employee" box on that form was checked, see page C-3 and check here ▶ [ ]	1	85,000.
2	Returns and allowances	2	
3	Subtract line 2 from line 1	3	85,000.
4	Cost of goods sold (from line 42 on page 2)	4	35,000.
5	**Gross profit.** Subtract line 4 from line 3	5	50,000.
6	Other income, including Federal and state gasoline or fuel tax credit or refund (see page C-3)	6	
7	**Gross income.** Add lines 5 and 6 ▶	7	50,000.

Part II   Expenses. Enter expenses for business use of your home **only** on line 30.

8	Advertising	8		19	Pension and profit-sharing plans	19	
9	Car and truck expenses (see page C-3)	9	3,600.	20	Rent or lease (see page C-5):		
				a	Vehicles, machinery, and equipment	20a	
10	Commissions and fees	10		b	Other business property	20b	
11	Contract labor (see page C-4)	11		21	Repairs and maintenance	21	
12	Depletion	12		22	Supplies (not included in Part III)	22	
13	Depreciation and section 179 expense deduction (not included in Part III) (see page C-4)	13		23	Taxes and licenses	23	75.
				24	Travel, meals, and entertainment:		
14	Employee benefit programs (other than on line 19)	14		a	Travel	24a	8,000.
				b	Meals and entertainment	4,000.	
15	Insurance (other than health)	15		c	Enter nondeductible amount included on line 24b (see page C-5)	2,000.	
16	Interest:			d	Subtract line 24c from line 24b	24d	2,000.
a	Mortgage (paid to banks, etc.)	16a		25	Utilities	25	
b	Other	16b		26	Wages (less employment credits)	26	
17	Legal and professional services	17	350.	27	Other expenses (from line 48 on page 2)	27	2,435.
18	Office expense	18	275.				

28	**Total expenses** before expenses for business use of home. Add lines 8 through 27 in columns ▶	28	16,735.
29	Tentative profit (loss). Subtract line 28 from line 7	29	33,265.
30	Expenses for business use of your home. Attach Form 8829	30	
31	**Net profit or (loss).** Subtract line 30 from line 29.		
	• If a profit, enter on **Form 1040, line 12,** and **also** on **Schedule SE, line 2** (statutory employees, see page C-6). Estates and trusts, enter on Form 1041, line 3.	31	33,265.
	• If a loss, you **must** go to line 32.		
32	If you have a loss, check the box that describes your investment in this activity (see page C-6).		
	• If you checked 32a, enter the loss on **Form 1040, line 12,** and **also** on **Schedule SE, line 2** (statutory employees, see page C-6). Estates and trusts, enter on Form 1041, line 3.	32a [ ] All investment is at risk.	
	• If you checked 32b, you **must** attach Form 6198.	32b [ ] Some investment is not at risk.	

LHA   **For Paperwork Reduction Act Notice, see Form 1040 instructions.**   Schedule C (Form 1040)

420001   11-03-04

Example 7:

Schedule C (Form 1040)   HARRY JONES   777-88-9999 Page **2**

Part III | **Cost of Goods Sold** (see page C-6)

33 Method(s) used to
value closing inventory: **a** ☐ Cost   **b** ☐ Lower of cost or market   **c** ☐ Other (attach explanation)

34 Was there any change in determining quantities, costs, or valuations between opening and closing inventory? If
"Yes," attach explanation .... ☐ Yes   ☐ No

35 Inventory at beginning of year. If different from last year's closing inventory, attach explanation	**35**	
36 Purchases less cost of items withdrawn for personal use	**36**	
37 Cost of labor. Do not include any amounts paid to yourself	**37**	
38 Materials and supplies	**38**	
39 Other costs	**39**	35,000.
40 Add lines 35 through 39	**40**	35,000.
41 Inventory at end of year	**41**	
42 **Cost of goods sold.** Subtract line 41 from line 40. Enter the result here and on page 1, line 4	**42**	35,000.

Part IV | **Information on Your Vehicle.** Complete this part **only** if you are claiming car or truck expenses on line 9 and are not required
to file Form 4562 for this business. See the instructions for line 13 on page C-4 to find out if you must file Form 4562.

43 When did you place your vehicle in service for business purposes? (month, day, year) ▶ 01/01/04.

44 Of the total number of miles you drove your vehicle during 2004, enter the number of miles you used your vehicle for:

a Business _____ 9,600 _____ **b** Commuting _____ **c** Other _____ 5,400

45 Do you (or your spouse) have another vehicle available for personal use? .... ☒ Yes   ☐ No

46 Was your vehicle available for personal use during off-duty hours? .... ☒ Yes   ☐ No

47 a Do you have evidence to support your deduction? .... ☒ Yes   ☐ No
b If "Yes," is the evidence written? .... ☒ Yes   ☐ No

Part V | **Other Expenses.** List below business expenses not included on lines 8-26 or line 30.

BANK CHARGES	60.
BOOKS	250.
BANK CHARGES	25.
CELL PHONE	1,500.
INTERNET FEES	600.
48 Total other expenses. Enter here and on page 1, line 27	**48**	2,435.

420002/ 11-03-04   Schedule C (Form 1040)

109

Example 7:

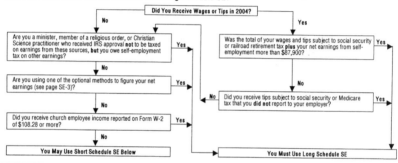

SCHEDULE SE
(Form 1040)

Department of the Treasury
Internal Revenue Service

Self-Employment Tax

OMB No. 1545-0074

▶ Attach to Form 1040. ▶ See Instructions for Schedule SE (Form 1040).

Attachment
Sequence No. **17**

Name of person with **self-employment** income (as shown on Form 1040)

HARRY JONES

Social security number of
person with **self-employment**
income ▶ 777 88 9999

Who Must File Schedule SE

You must file Schedule SE if:

- You had net earnings from self-employment from **other than** church employee income (line 4 of Short Schedule SE or line 4c of Long Schedule SE) of $400 or more **or**

- You had church employee income of $108.28 or more. Income from services you performed as a minister or a member of a religious order **is not** church employee income (see page SE-1).

Note. Even if you had a loss or a small amount of income from self-employment, it may be to your benefit to file Schedule SE and use either "optional method" in Part II of Long Schedule SE (see page SE-3).

Exception. If your only self-employment income was from earnings as a minister, member of a religious order, or Christian Science practitioner **and** you filed Form 4361 and received IRS approval not to be taxed on those earnings, **do not** file Schedule SE. Instead, write "Exempt-Form 4361" on Form 1040, line 57.

May I Use Short Schedule SE or Must I Use Long Schedule SE?

Did You Receive Wages or Tips in 2004?

No →

Are you a minister, member of a religious order, or Christian Science practitioner who received IRS approval **not** to be taxed on earnings from these sources, **but** you owe self-employment tax on other earnings? → Yes ▶

No ↓

Are you using one of the optional methods to figure your net earnings (see page SE-3)? → Yes ▶

No ↓

Did you receive church employee income reported on Form W-2 of $108.28 or more? → Yes ▶

No ↓

You May Use Short Schedule SE Below

Yes →

Was the total of your wages and tips subject to social security or railroad retirement tax **plus** your net earnings from self-employment more than $87,900? → Yes ▶

No ↓

Did you receive tips subject to social security or Medicare tax that you **did not** report to your employer? ← No / Yes ▶

You Must Use Long Schedule SE

Section A-Short Schedule SE. Caution. Read above to see if you can use Short Schedule SE.

1 Net farm profit or (loss) from Schedule F, line 36, and farm partnerships, Schedule K-1 (Form 1065), box 14, code A	1	
2 Net profit or (loss) from Schedule C, line 31; Schedule C-EZ, line 3; Schedule K-1 (Form 1065), box 14, code A (other than farming); and Schedule K-1 (Form 1065-B), box 9. Ministers and members of religious orders, see page SE-1 for amounts to report on this line. See page SE-2 for other income to report	2	33,265.
3 Combine lines 1 and 2	3	33,265.
4 **Net earnings from self-employment.** Multiply line 3 by 92.35% (.9235). If less than $400, **do not** file this schedule; you do not owe self-employment tax ▶	4	30,720.
5 **Self-employment tax.** If the amount on line 4 is: • $87,900 or less, multiply line 4 by 15.3% (.153). Enter the result here and on **Form 1040, line 57.** • More than $87,900, multiply line 4 by 2.9% (.029). Then, add $10,899.60 to the result. Enter the total here and on **Form 1040, line 57.**	5	4,700.
6 **Deduction for one-half of self-employment tax.** Multiply line 5 by 50% (.5). Enter the result here and on **Form 1040, line 30**	6	2,350.

LHA **For Paperwork Reduction Act Notice, see Form 1040 instructions.**

Schedule SE (Form 1040)

424501
10-27-04

I hope these examples have helped you to see what can happen with your tax return. It is important to know as much as you can because missing a deduction can make a tremendous difference on your tax return.

Again, it is best to consult with a professional that may know a few more tax laws than you will able to learn on your own.

YOU'VE GOT QUESTIONS?
I'VE GOT ANSWERS!

♠ ♥ ♣ ♦

Over the past several years, people have asked questions that I thought would be best addressed in a Q&A section in case you want a "fast" answer. Here are a few.

CAN I TAKE LOSSES FROM MY GAMBLING BUSINESS?

No, if your gambling falls into the definition of a business, you can only deduct expenses up to your losses. The IRS currently is not allowing gamblers to take more than their winnings off their tax return.

I AM A PRO. CAN I INCORPORATE MYSELF INTO A BUSINESS TO SAVE SOME OF THE SELF-EMPLOYMENT TAXES? I WOULD LIKE TO BE A CORPORATION.

A person that is a professional gambler cannot incorporate themselves. There are many court cases where professional athletes have wanted to do this. The IRS feels that you are a personal service that you cannot have anyone else perform, such as Michael Jordan cannot get someone to take his place. The same goes with a pro that is not able to "substitute" their ability with someone else.

WHAT IF I DO A GAMBLING-RELATED BUSINESS, SUCH AS SELLING POKER CHIPS?

That is different. You can file this on a Schedule C with your personal return and you can take losses on this. Remember, the only business where you cannot take losses is gambling or wagering. See Chapter 10 for more on this.

CAN I REPORT MY INCOME ON A MONTHLY BASIS TO THE IRS?

The IRS doesn't want to know the particulars about your income during the year. That is your responsibility to keep up with. They do, however, want you to pay in your taxes during the year based on your income. This is called estimate payments which can be paid on or before 4/15, 6/15, 9/15, or 1/15 of the year following the tax year that you are paying. This is submitted on a Form 1040-ES. Don't forget that if you live in a State that has a State Income Tax, you need to also pay into that State. Your best bet is to call your State Department of Revenue and they can tell you the form to submit.

MY POKER IS A HOBBY. I LOVE TO GO TO DIFFERENT CITIES AND PLAY IN TOURNAMENTS. I HAVE WON TOURNAMENTS THAT TOTAL ABOUT $5,000. THE COST OF MY HOTELS, PLANE TICKETS AND MEALS WERE SUBSTANTIAL. CAN I OFFSET THESE EXPENSES AGAINST MY $5,000 OF INCOME?

No, see Chapter 3. You can only deduct your gambling losses, not expenses if you are a hobby. Keep a poker log, as in Chapter 8, to make sure you keep up with your wagering losses to offset the income. You can also download this on my web site at **www.pokerdeductions.com**.

NOT ONLY DO I PLAY POKER PROFESSIONALLY, I ALSO PLAY BLACKJACK AND DO SPORTS BETTING. CAN I FILE ALL OF THIS INCOME TOGETHER ON MY TAX RETURN?

Yes, all of this is under the same category of gambling. You can file all of this income, and the related expenses, under your Schedule C (Profit of Loss from Business) with your personal tax return (Form 1040).

WHAT WOULD BE THE BEST WAY TO KEEP RECORDS ON MY PLAY AND SHOULD THESE RECORDS INCLUDE SOME FORM OF PROOF FROM THE CASINO?

If you plan on writing off your wagering, you need to somehow keep a record of this. I have an example in the book and you can also visit my website at www.pokerdeductions.com for a download of this. There is really not any "proof" from the casino. You could get someone to initial the day's play but I really don't think it is necessary if you are keeping a detailed log.

CAN I DEDUCT MY TOURNAMENT ENTRY FEES?

Yes, you can deduct this as part of your wagering expenses.

DO I HAVE TO POSSESS A TAX STAMP FOR GAMBLING?

The IRS does not require such a stamp. However, check with the State that you live in. State laws vary from Federal laws and may require such.

WHAT CAN I WRITE OFF AS EXPENSES IF I AM A PRO?

The best thing to do is look at Chapter 5, to best explain this in more detail.

I AM A PRO SO THEREFORE I AM SELF-EMPLOYED. WHAT CAN I DO, IF ANYTHING, TO SAVE FOR RETIREMENT?

The best thing for you to do is read Chapter 9 which will explain various retirement plans and options. As a professional gambler, you can set up retirement plans just as any other business does.

I HOST POKER GAMES AND TOURNAMENTS AT MY HOUSE. I SPEND A LOT OF MONEY BUYING CHIPS, CARDS, ETC. CAN I WRITE OFF ANY OF THIS?

Home games for gambling need to be looked as whether it is a hobby or a business. You really need to ask yourself the questions in Chapter 2 to see where you fall.

I DID NOT REPORT MY GAMBLING WINNINGS AND LOSSES ON MY 2004 TAX RETURN. WHAT SHOULD I DO?

You have three years to file an Amended Return on a Form 1040X. The sooner you do this the better, especially if you are going to owe additional tax to lessen the penalty and interest.

I WON MONEY AT A TOURNAMENT IN PARIS AND ON A CRUISE SHIP. DO I HAVE TO REPORT THIS ON MY TAX RETURN?

Yes, gambling winnings that occur outside the United States are not exempt from taxes. As a U.S. citizen, you are taxed on all of your income sources.

SINCE I GAMBLE AS A HOBBY, ARE MY WINNINGS SUBJECT TO THE SELF-EMPLOYMENT TAX?

No, gambling winnings are not considered earned income unless you are a professional gambler.

GLOSSARY OF TERMS

♠ ♥ ♣ ♦

Accelerated Depreciation: The act of taking depreciation at a greater than usual rate.

Accounting: The process of recording, classifying, reporting, and interpreting the financial data of an organization.

Accounting System: The principles, methods, and procedures relating to the incurrence, classification, recording, and reporting of the transactions of an organization.

Adjusted Gross Income: The amount used in the calculation of an individual's income tax liability; one's income after certain adjustments are made, but before standard or itemized deductions and personal exemptions are made.

Assets: Those economic resources of an entity that can usefully be expressed in monetary terms; some examples are cash, accounts receivable, inventories, and plant and equipment.

Balance Sheet: A financial report showing the financial position of an entity in terms of assets, liabilities, and owners' equity at a specific date.

Budgeting: A process of formal financial planning.

Capital Expense: An expense intended to benefit future periods, in contrast to a revenue expenditure which benefits a current period.

Cash Basis: A form of accounting where revenue is recognized only when the money is received and expenses are recognized when the money is paid.

Conservatism: An accounting principle stating that you should lean toward understatement rather than overstatement of assets and income.

Corporation: A legal entity created by the granting of a charter from an appropriate governmental authority and owned by stockholders.

Cost of Goods Sold: The cost of merchandise sold to customers during the accounting period. It is calculated by adding the beginning inventory and net cost of purchases and deducting the ending inventory.

CPA: Certified Public Accountant, a professional accountant who has passed the Uniform CPA Examination, satisfied other requirements regarding education, professional experience, and character, and been licensed to practice public accounting by a state, district, or territory.

Crying Call: Calling a hand when you have a very low chance of winning; the call you make to the accountant when you find out the IRS is auditing your tax return.

Current Assets: Assets that will either be used up or converted to cash within the normal operating cycle of the business or one year, whichever is longer.

Depreciation: The decline in value of assets originating from wear, deterioration, and obsolescence.

Depreciation Expense: That portion of an asset that is recognized as having expired and thus is an expense.

Earned Income: Compensation from participation in a business, including wages, salaries, commissions, etc.

Entity: A division of the activities of a person, partnership, corporation or other organization, separate and complete in form.

Expenses: Costs incurred by business in the process of earning revenue.

FICA Taxes: FICA is a term used to denote both the Social Security and Medicare taxes upon earned income whose combined rate for both the employer and employee is 15.3% in 2004. The tax is upon earned as opposed to passive income such as dividends, interest and other investment income. FICA taxes are reported for employees on IRS form 941 and, for self-employed individuals, upon Schedule SE to form 1040. Form 941 is filed quarterly whereas form Schedule SE is filed annually. For self-employed individuals, the terms "FICA tax" and "self-employment tax" are synonymous.

Fish: A bad poker player; who you will be swimming with if you skip town owing money and they find you.

Flush: Five cards of the same suit; what your face does if you miss-deal at your home game.

Going Home Hand: A hand where a poker player wagers his last chips or money; the hand attached to the thumb you use to hitch a ride when the IRS takes your car.

Gross profit: Calculated as sales minus all costs directly related to those sales. These costs can include manufacturing expenses, raw materials, labor, selling, marketing and other expenses.

High Society: A stack of $10,000; where you will be mingling if you make lots of money playing poker.

IRS: The Internal Revenue Service of the Federal government, primarily responsible for applying the current tax codes and regulations and collecting income taxes; can also stand for "I'm really screwed" if you are caught cheating on your tax return.

Juice: Interest on the money that you borrow; also orange, grapefruit and pineapple.

Liabilities: Present obligations resulting from past transactions that require the firm to pay money, provide goods, or perform services in the future.

Maniac: A very aggressive player who is always raising the pot and playing every hand; someone who deducts expenses on his tax return that are not deductible.

Net Income: In business, what remains after subtracting all the costs (namely, business, depreciation, interest, and taxes) from a company's revenues, Net income is sometimes called the bottom line. This is also referred to as earnings or net profit. For an individual, gross income minus taxes, allowances, and deductions. An individual's net income is used to determine how much income tax is owed.

Placed in Service: When something is available for use in your work or business or in an income-producing activity.

Profit and Loss Statement: The difference between income and expenses of a business for a period and the profit (or loss) resulting from it.

Proprietorship: A form of business organization in which one person owns the business; sometimes termed sole proprietorship.

Realized: Revenue is realized when the goods or services are exchanged for cash.

Street: A betting round, such as flop, turn or river; where you will be living if the IRS catches you cheating on your tax return.

Tax Evasion: A deliberate misstatement of factors determining taxable income. Tax evasion is illegal and subjects the taxpayer to legal prosecution.

Taxable Income: The amount of income subject to income taxes; your gross income minus all adjustments, deductions and exemptions.

Under the Gun: The first player to act preflop in early position; the place you will be if you don't repay the money you borrowed.

Unearned Income: An individual's income derived from sources other than employment, such as interest, dividends, income from rental property, capital gains, etc.

ABOUT THE AUTHOR

♠ ♥ ♣ ♦

Ann-Margaret Johnston is a native and life-long resident of Georgia. She received her Bachelor's degree in Accounting from Clayton College and State University. She is a Certified Public Accountant and a member of the Georgia Society of CPA's. She has worked in the field of accounting since 1986 and began her accounting practice in 1995. She has been a Rotarian for 10 years and is active in her local Rotary club.

In 1997, she took her first trip to Vegas. She became intrigued with Texas Hold'em poker and took a lesson in a popular Las Vegas casino. Ever since, she has been playing poker for the pure enjoyment and the challenge of the game in Las Vegas, Tunica, Atlantic City, Biloxi, Wisconsin, Canada, on-line and any other chance she gets. She has won several small tournaments and poker is her favorite subject to discuss.

Her parents live in Georgia and her father has been the Atlanta Braves photographer for the past 39 years and is a Normandy survivor.

Ann-Margaret's other interests include traveling, scuba diving, boating, wine, and cooking.

By choice, she has no children of her own, but has a wonderful step-daughter, Sherra, that lives in New York. Ann-Margaret and her husband David live on a lake in North Georgia with "Madison", their West Highland Terrier.

Ann-Margaret can be found on several internet poker sites under the name "CPAEvil".

NOTES:

NOTES:

NOTES:

NOTES:

NOTES: